Marigold Girls™

To my amazing "little" family with more gratitude and love than my words could ever express.

For my patient husband, Peter, who keeps it together each day, even with the household deficit of testosterone. Our roller coaster has been the best anyone could ever imagine and I am so glad we get to ride in the front seat together.

For my four sources of female inspiration; Priscilla, Sabrina, Presley and Frankie. Without you, this passion would have not been ignited. You help me focus on making this world a better place each day and bring me joy and love beyond imagination.

CONTENTS

INTRODUCTION

You, along with all the other girls in your life, are in the midst of finding a way to achieve a balance between who you are becoming and the emerging selves of those around you.

The subtitle of this book is "Growing our true selves and nurturing true friends by understanding the language of self and others." It means that in order to be comfortable in your own skin and develop healthy relationships, your goal is to discover the "how" and "why" girls act the way that they do. You will then be able to successfully navigate social behaviors like the pressure of popularity, by seeing things through a different lens. When you are able to step outside of the crazy girl stuff going on around you, and understand why things are going on, it's easier to stay authentic to YOU and not become someone else to be included.

"INNER GAMMA"

The term "Gamma Girl" is referenced in quite a few articles and books about relational aggression (you may know this as "mean girls") and stems from some terms related to the Greek alphabet to describe different types of girls as they move into puberty and adolescence. Initially, this book was going to be titled, *Gamma Girls*, but a Gamma Girl is focused on her authentic self (more on that later), and that is hard to start off with if you don't yet understand the social language of girls in your circles. So, let's break the types down and show you how we relate them to the elements in *our* garden. You will probably recognize these types easily!

The Alpha Girl is our Walnut Tree Girl!

The first letter in the Greek alphabet is Alpha and this first position describes the Alpha Girl perfectly. She is one who is always the leader, can be intimidating, and usually does what she needs to in order to be in front or on top. This is the "popular girl". The one who usually is portrayed as the mean girl in the movies. The girl that has the best clothes, the quarterback boyfriend, and does whatever she needs to in order to keep her #1 rank in the popular group. Alpha Girls wield a social power with others that usually includes some form of exclusivity. You may hear that term a lot in this book, so let's define it.

Exclusivity means to exclude (or keep you out) of something. This can be a group, club, friendship, etc. The Alpha Girls are part of a group that others want to be in that excludes others or isolates people they may find threatening for some reason. The tricky part is that these girls are usually well liked (or well feared). Many times, even if they are mean, they have quite a social following which is powerful in your teen years. We will come back to why that might be in later chapters.

Beta Girls are our Weeds, Daisies, Daffodils and Snowdrops!

The second letter in the Greek alphabet is Beta. It is fitting that this is the second letter, the one right behind the Alpha, she is always second in line but trying to make it to the front. Beta Girls are usually kind girls at heart who constantly try to keep up and fit in with the Alpha. In the mean girl movies, these girls are the "sidekick" or the "wanna be". She is the one that always does the dirty work for the Alpha Girl, but you kind of know deep down that she is a kind person that just wants to fit in. This tends to maker her do things that she may not normally do just to make sure she isn't the target of the Alpha's revenge.

The Gamma Girl is our MARIGOLD!

The Gamma Girl is described as the best version of girlhood. It may be the letter behind the other two in the alphabet, but in terms of relational aggression and how girls interact with each other, she stands alone. She is authentic and holds true to her own beliefs, morals, and values. Unlike the Alphas who tend to be about themselves, Gamma Girls tend to talk about activities they're doing for others. They are often very good at mingling with all sorts of groups and most people consider them a friend. They are not focused on trying to achieve popularity. Instead, their focus is on achieving goals they have set for themselves, pursuing interests outside of just moving up the social ladder.

SO, WHY A MARIGOLD?

When you think Marigold Girls ™, I'm sure your first thought might be that girls are blooming like a flower. GAG! This book is not about frilly frills. It's meant to shift perspective for girls, to help them see that they are not crazy and that the crap going on around them with their friends and other girls is REAL. The title didn't come from a "foo foo" idea of a flower blooming, instead it came from reading an article that I came across when I was working with teachers to help them be stronger in the classroom. It was meant to help teachers find support when they needed it as they started out in their career. However, the idea kept resonating with me, and as it grew, I started to develop ideas for how to write this book.

You see, it stems from the idea that marigolds are unique plants, not because they are tough and withstand any climate or torturous incident mother nature can present, but because when planted next to other bits of nature, they help them grow, become stronger, and survive themselves. Even a tree that secrets poison like the walnut tree. The walnut tree is a glorious tree; strong and beautiful. It produces yummy walnuts. However, in order for it to become that, it secures its place in the ground by secreting a toxic substance that kills many other plants around it....EXCEPT marigolds.

Marigold flowers are immune to the poison and not only live around the tree but support tree growth as well. There is NO competition like there is with other plants or trees surrounding the walnut. Instead, the Marigold is a companion plant that helps others ward off destructive pests! The title of this book came from this wondrous piece of nature because...

Marigolds do not die nourishing others plants.

They do not compete with other plants to be the most beautiful, or the strongest, or tallest.

They are companion plants that support other elements in the garden by protecting them.

So, the purpose of the title is to remind you that you can be the marigold. There is no need to compete with others or give up who you are as a sacrifice to grow and flourish. By being rooted in your own sense of self and sharing positively with boundaries, you can exist and grow even with a walnut tree next to you! This book is designed to help you develop into your own Marigold Girl™!

HOW TO USE THIS BOOK

Just a quick note about what you will find in this book and how to use it. In each chapter that you read you will find information about different topics related to relational aggression (mean girl behavior). After the information, you will be offered a few activities that you can use to help you think about what you have read and how it might fit into your life. These activities are just a way for you to explore the information in order to clarify your current situation with girls around you and your social situations. I would recommend trying at least one per chapter and you can always come back to them as things change in your social circles as well (a kind of refresher).

Lastly, you will find some questions at the end of each chapter. These questions are paired with journaling pages. One of the best ways to get clear about what is going on around you is to journal about it. The questions were developed to guide you in your journaling. Think of it as a way to kick-start your thoughts and insights about yourself and the girls around you. I would strongly encourage you to use this part and know that this is for you alone. If you have a trusted adult to share and discuss it with, that's even better, but really it is for you to just get your thoughts out on paper and start thinking about things after you have some information.

CHAPTER 1

What Is Relational Aggression and Where Does It Come From?

In her book, *Odd Girl Out*, Rachel Simmons sums it up best when she said, "Without an understanding of their unique experience of bullying, girls often end up blaming themselves for their own victimization." In other words, when you understand how it works, you understand that it is not really about YOU. Instead, you begin to shift the way you view things to see that the things the girls around you are saying and doing have a different purpose, something outside of you that is more primal in nature and really is more about THEM. That being said, just because you know it isn't truly about you doesn't mean it is easy to deal with so, at the end of this book you will also find some tips and tricks. Things to help you navigate and manage some of the emotional ups and downs that come with dealing with girls during adolescence and beyond.

DIFFERENT TYPES OF AGGRESSION

Before we launch into the main type of aggression that this book is about, it is important for you to understand the different types of aggression. Many times aggressive acts are not black and white. In most circumstances you will see a mixture of different aggressive types when someone uses them. If you are able to understand what each one looks like, it is easier to identify then when you see them happening in real life situations.

Direct Aggression

Direct aggression is not hidden. This type is either physical or verbal. It happens to a person and is clearly happening. Some examples of direct aggression can be physically fighting, pushing, yelling at someone in person or through digital format (texting, social media, etc). Whatever it is, it is out there and people know that one person is attacking another.

Indirect (Secret) Aggression

Unlike direct aggression, indirect aggression is much more difficult to call out. It is hidden and involves one person targeting another but doing it in a way that is not necessarily person-to-person. It usually involves a third party or hidden acts (physical or verbal). Some examples include spreading anonymous rumors, gossiping behind the person's back, posting mean things on social media, etc.

Social Aggression

Social aggression is really an umbrella that involves a number of different types listed here (relational, indirect (secret), and nonverbal). It is about lowering someone else's self-esteem and knocking them down the popularity ladder. This can be done by using insults, body language, facial expressions, and such. This isn't the exact form of relational aggression that involves rumors and other things. Instead, you might see someone rolling their eyes when you come around or tossing their hair and then turning to walk away when you try to talk to them. They don't necessarily say anything, to you or anyone else, but the nonverbal cues they give and even small sounds (scoffs, and mumbling) tell a story to others that you are not worthy of their time. This type of aggression eats at a girl's self esteem because the aggressive acts are hard to identify and share with others yet, at the same time, it is VERY clear that they are happening to you. Many times, this is the first stage in relational aggression.

RELATIONAL AGGRESSION

Relational aggression has different definitions but the theme that is the same in all of them is that it involves aggression with the intent to harm relationships through manipulation. *What does that really mean???* Basically, it means that someone sets out to manipulate or control you by making you feel bad about yourself or your friendships with others. They also can try to control how others see you or think of you by making you feel alone and not part of a group. This is called exclusion and the isolation is a hallmark trait of relational aggression. The main feature of relational aggressive behavior is when someone uses their relationships to hurt other people. Researchers have found that this can be done in a few different ways; social, direct and/or indirect.[1]

Here is what these might look like...

Direct Aggression:
Claire tells Jane that she isn't allowed to sit with the group at the lunch table unless she brings them all a soda.

Indirect Aggression:
Claire starts a rumor at school that Jane had her period at school and that is why she was absent for three days.

Social Aggression (exclusion):
Jane walks up to the lunch table to sit with the "popular" group and as soon as she sits down the group gets up and moves to another table.

Girls usually will use relational aggression in a covert (or secret) way. They can target someone individually or focus on a bigger picture with a girl's social status in a group. Most of the time these things happen at school, since this is where the majority of your social time is spent. Although, if you have a strong social life outside of school you can also see these things pop up there.

Indirect or "secret" aggression is the type you will probably experience the most, so let's dig into it a bit more. This is the hardest for people to see and explain. It usually involves someone doing something to someone

1. Bjoerkqvist

else "in secret". Rachel Simmons explains in her book *Odd Girl Out*, "It isn't just about not getting caught; half of it is looking like you'd never mistreat someone in the first place." When someone uses this type, they work hard at using a "good girl reputation" to hide behind. Teachers and other adults around them think they would never do anything mean to others so they use this as a cover. This lets them to do things like bump into you in the hallway then say, "Watch where you are going" or knock the book you are reading off your desk as they walk by then smile at your and say, "Oops, sorry." This is when the social aggressive acts start and can continue to grow.

One of the biggest frustrations with girls that fall victim to this kind of aggression is that they might tell a teacher or other adult and not be believed because the adults never see the aggressive acts. The adults only see the "good" side of the person being mean.

BULLYING VERSUS AGGRESSIVE BEHAVIOR

Is it possible for someone to show aggressive behavior and not be a bully? The answer is YES! There may be people that you know who have done a few things here or there who were mean to others, maybe even intentional (on purpose). Usually, this happens with people in the group who are trying to avoid being kicked out, isolated or preserve their own feelings. They are not excessively mean, but just had a few moments of bad judgement trying to find their way to fit in.

On the other hand, bullying is when the aggression is happening regularly. You can see a pattern of behavior that is happening with one person and they are doing things repeatedly to hurt someone else; they have a target. When this is happening it is important to seek help from trusted adults around you because bullying can cause long-term emotional damage.

WHERE DOES ALL THIS COME FROM?

Without getting too deep on you, it is important to know that there are some biological reasons that have been discussed that explain why these things are happening. Research suggests that women and men play different roles in society. This stems back to the beginning of human existence, when men were the hunters and gatherers and women's role was to protect their young in order to continue creating other humans.

Previously, researchers found that when presented with something that was threatening (and caused fear or anxiety) a person would respond with FIGHT, FLIGHT (leave as quickly as possible) or FREEZE. If you think about the last time you were really scared by something you might remember falling into one of these categories. It is an automatic response from your body to keep you safe, stemming back to caveman days.

Fast forward to where we are today and researchers have discussed applying similar principles. The theory goes that when a woman does not belong to a social circle, it may be putting her safety (and that of her children) at risk because they wouldn't have people to support them. This would ultimately isolate them, making it difficult to survive on their own. Additionally, if they are targeted as unworthy of being loved, they may not be attractive to another partner, which would jeopardize their ability to continue creating humans. Some research has also suggested that women show certain physical signs (increased heart rate) when they start to feel rejected from social situations[2]. This also supports the theory that women need to keep their social relationships strong.

2. Benenson, 2013

Basically, this theory says that women also have a primal need to belong that is not just for themselves but goes back to the days when they HAD to have a group around them in order to survive. This need is so ingrained in our DNA that it takes over to this day even though we are no longer cavemen.

However, newer research has noted that girls and women respond to stress differently than boys and men. Shelley Taylor, Ph.D., and her colleagues, studied stress responses from females and found that instead of the traditional fight/flight/freeze model, females move toward a "tend and befriend" model. This is the idea that when under stress, women "tend to" or move their focus to taking care of their children and young ones instead of fighting or leaving. The most interesting part that relates to relational aggression, is that they also have a tendency to want to be around other familiar people more during times of stress.

So what does this have to do with you and your "mean girl" friends? Well, here is the thing, if you take this model into account, you can see that when you are under stress from someone targeting you through relational aggression, as a female, you seek out other people to help you feel better (befriending). However, since the main focus of relational aggression is to find ways to isolate you and exclude you from certain social circles, it makes it harder for you to do that. This increases your stress even more. When this happens it cuts into a deep part of our caveman brain and makes us feel desperate. Many times, this can explain why girls begin to move toward other ways of coping, like hurting themselves, using drugs, or drinking.

MEAN GIRL ISOLATES YOU, WHICH CAUSES STRESS.

YOU GO TO FRIENDS BUT HAVE BEEN KICKED OUT OF THE GROUP, WHICH CAUSES MORE STRESS.

THIS LEADS TO FEELING DESPERATE AND ALONE.

When you understand this concept, it becomes easier to see when you might be moving into this desperate mode because you now have an understanding of why you might be feeling this crazy way. It is normal to feel a little desperate when you are cut off from social circles because your mammalian brain is scared to death that you won't survive. But...

YOUR MODERN—THINKING BRAIN CAN TAKE OVER AND CALM THIS PART DOWN

ONCE YOU REALIZE THAT THERE ARE OTHER WAYS TO BE CONNECTED OUTSIDE OF

THIS ONE SOCIAL CIRCLE.

ACTIVITIES

1. Interview a man and woman (that you trust and are close to) using the following questions to see if there is a difference in how they react to stress:

MAN

When was the last time you were really scared or embarrassed?

_____

_____

_____

What did you do?

_____

_____

_____

WOMAN

When was the last time you were really scared or embarrassed?

_____

_____

_____

What did you do?

_____

_____

_____

2. Think of when someone in your social circle made you feel threatened (embarrassed or scared). Dissect how you reacted to this stress.

Describe the scenario:

_____

_____

_____

How did you react?

FIGHT? OR FLIGHT? OR FREEZE? OR TEND? OR BEFRIEND?
Debate!   *Run away!*   *Do nothing!*   *Take care of!*   *Make friends!*

_____

_____

_____

Now imagine the scene again and think about these questions:
- What was your immediate thought when it happened?
- What was the feeling you had next?
- Do you think your thought led to your feeling in any way? How?

3. Use the table below to write some of your old thoughts and feelings. Now try to see them through a different lens. See if a new perspective might change the outcome of future challenges that may arise.

OLD THOUGHT	OLD FEELING	NEW THOUGHT	NEW FEELING

JOURNALING QUESTIONS

1. What kind of things have you seen others do around you that involve using indirect (secret) aggression?

_____

_____

_____

_____

_____

_____

_____

2. Have you ever known someone that has been bullied, even if it was you? Did you know it was bullying at the time? What made you realize it? Did you do anything about it? Why or why not?

_____

_____

_____

_____

_____

_____

_____

3. Spend some time over the next week observing people at school. Can you spot the three types of girls in the social circles there? Who are the Alpha, Beta and Gamma Girls? How can you tell?

_____

_____

_____

_____

_____

_____

_____

4. Where do you fit into your social circle?

_____

_____

_____

_____

_____

_____

_____

5. Do you see any of the types of aggression we just learned about happening in your own social circles? What do the situations look like?

_____

_____

_____

_____

_____

_____

_____

_____

_____

_____

_____

_____

_____

_____

_____

_____

_____

CHAPTER 2
The Garden Of Friendship

You will find that throughout this book there are a lot of references to gardens (in addition to the walnut trees and marigolds). These were chosen because of the overlapping themes they have in common with friendships and relationships. For the majority of this book we will be talking about marigolds and walnut trees (as referenced in the beginning of the book). However, before we launch into that let's chat for a moment about gardens and friendships.

Gardens can include a variety of things: flower, plants, vegetables, fruits, even succulents. It really doesn't matter what type of plant is in the garden, in each of them there is usually a variation of plants. There are big dominant plants that demand more sunlight and food than other smaller plants; there are plants that are thorny and others that lend a hand to the other plants by keeping away certain insects that could harm them. The type of soil they grow in either helps or harms the plants. Gardens are intricate and complicated and so much like the friendships and relationships we have in our lives.

Take a minute to think about the friends in your garden.

Can you fit any of them into the descriptions above? My guess is that you can. We all have a friend who is the life of the party, dominating conversations and always wanting the spotlight to shine on them. Or how about that friend who is quiet and shy but always there to help others? You might even have a friend who can sap all your energy just by being around them too long? On the opposite side of that coin could be a friend who makes you feel alive and powerful. They are always positive and supporting you, which makes you feel good each time they are around.

A garden has a variety of elements that make it work, some are more beneficial and effective than others. Friendships and cliques are the same. The people you surround yourself with are the pieces of your garden. They can either empower us and make us feel better, working at a higher level and feeling strong, or they can drag us down and make us feel bad about ourselves, isolating us from others and make us fear being alone and not a part of the group.

DO THEY HAVE TO BE ONE OR THE OTHER?

Well, that answer can get a little more complicated because as you will see later, we really all have a bit of both the marigold and the walnut tree inside us. We make the decision through knowledge and experience to embrace the marigold status as a way of thinking and being. So there are many people in your group that may one day stand with you in marigold country while the next day be trying to take over your soil as a walnut tree.

The point is not that you should try to change them. Instead, you use recognition of this process and understanding of when this might be happening, because knowledge is power. Having the knowledge to be able to see what is happening helps you to navigate your role and stand strong as a marigold regardless of other people's choices.

There are some of us who have more than one clique or group that we hang out with and that is ok too. What I want you to think about is how your garden is laid out in each of these groups. The groups may be very different (just like a variation of gardens) but, more than likely, each of these groups has at least one Walnut tree that you will recognize. Usually you will recognize this person as the one that tends to manipulate others in the group and rise to the top of the social ladder. This person may have just been planted and doesn't seem to have strong roots yet (so it isn't quite as clear that she is it) or she may have long strong roots and clearly be the person who is running the show. Either way, by understanding who is involved in your groups you empower yourself to see things from a different perspective.

HOW THEY WORK TOGETHER

You learned in the introduction of this book that marigolds and walnut trees can live together and both still survive and thrive despite the toxic substance a walnut tree produces. However, in our garden (that includes walnut trees and marigolds) it is important to remember that even though they CAN coexist and support each other, they can also each live WITHOUT each other. If the marigolds were not planted around the walnut tree it would continue to grow, dominating the plants around it and getting stronger and stronger, until it took over the garden and was the only tree left. Likewise, the marigold would continue to support other, different plants in a different garden, finding ways to grow with others.

This is an important note to store in your memory banks because it may be that within your circles you find a Walnut Tree Girl who is one you choose NOT to be planted with in your garden. You may find that there is a particular friend that falls in that category and, despite your Marigold ways, they continue to poison the circle of friends. The tough part about co-existing with a Walnut Tree (from a Marigold's perspective) is that unless you have other Marigolds in your garden, it can be a tough road. The hope is that through the act of being a Marigold Girl, you will shine a light on the positive aspects of compassion, integrity, honesty, and authenticity, so others will want to rise to meet you. However, if the walnut tree has already taken hold with strong roots, you may choose to leave instead.

Always give yourself permission to leave a garden!

LEAVING A CIRCLE OF FRIENDS IS NEVER EASY, BUT THERE ARE WAYS TO DISTANCE YOURSELF BY SPENDING TIME WITH OTHER GROUPS. EVENTUALLY, YOU WILL FIND YOUR WAY OUT OF THE OLD GARDEN AND PLANT SOME STRONGER ROOTS IN ONE THAT IS MORE SUPPORTIVE OF YOUR MARIGOLD STATUS.

The truth is, if the girl who falls into Walnut Tree status is not willing to make change, they will eventually poison the others around them one by one. You will then see people chose to either leave the group, or choose to stay and be unhappy in order to be a part of the group.

ACTIVITIES

Now that you have learned a little about the garden of friendship, stop for a minute and try these activities to learn how your garden is made up.

1. Think about the groups of people you hang out with and then group them into the bubbles below (add more if needed). You may have a number of different groups you are involved with: academic groups, sports groups, friends from forever, new friends, etc. *These are your surrounding cliques and make up your garden. Take a moment to think about each person in that group and identify if they are more of a marigold or a walnut tree in your life at the moment. (Some may fall in the middle and into more of that "Beta Girl" category. If that is the case just place a star next to their name because we will talk about them later.)*

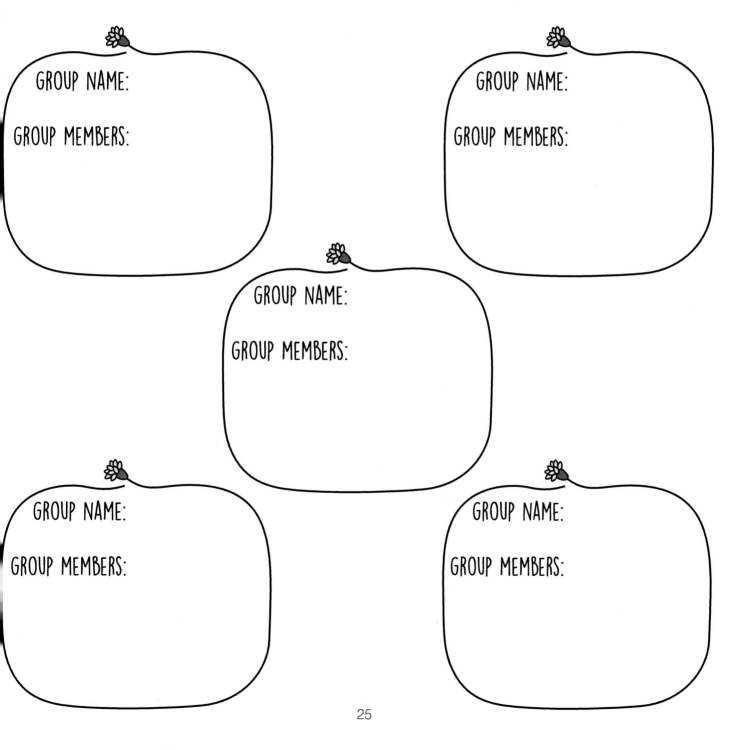

GROUP NAME:

GROUP MEMBERS:

GROUP NAME:

GROUP MEMBERS:

GROUP NAME:

GROUP MEMBERS:

GROUP NAME:

GROUP MEMBERS:

GROUP NAME:

GROUP MEMBERS:

2.   Now that you have identified the elements of your garden, think about this. The groups that you are involved with all have their own distinct culture. What do I mean by that? Well...think of it as the unwritten rules of the group. Rules that everyone seems to know but no one really ever says out loud. These are things like:

YOU HAVE TO WEAR A CERTAIN TYPE OF CLOTHING.
YOU CAN'T TALK OR HANG WITH CERTAIN TYPES OF PEOPLE.
YOU CAN BE SMART BUT DON'T FLAUNT IT.
IF YOU HAVE MONEY YOU ARE TREATED BETTER AND MORE RESPECTED.

These are the things that none of us like to admit, but are real unwritten rules in certain groups. Depending on your group, these unwritten rules may be different.

So, using the groups you identified, what are some of the unwritten rules of each of the groups you listed? Take a moment to use the lines next to each bubble to write down some of the unwritten rules for each one.

GROUP NAME:

GROUP NAME:

GROUP NAME:

GROUP NAME:

GROUP NAME:

Now that you have dissected your groups a little, think about this...what role do you play in each of these groups? See, the thing is that your participation in each of these groups helps it to stay alive. Sometimes it is hard to admit our role if it is not flattering or we have made some choices that may have hurt others (either directly or indirectly). On the opposite side of the spectrum, it may be that you have been the victim of someone else in one of these groups. You may also find that you play a different role in different groups. In one group you are victim and in the other you are leader. None of it is right or wrong; it is just a way for you to start to recognize your role and other's roles in the groups you have surrounding you.

SO HOW DO THESE UNWRITTEN RULES IMPACT YOU?

Well, if you don't follow the unwritten rules, you can start to feel threatened that you will not be a part of the group anymore. When this happens, the idea of being alone is one of the scariest thoughts, especially in school. In the book *Queen Bees and Wannabe's*, the author talks about how cliques are "self-reinforcing." What she meant by that is that when you become a part of a group you gain a role. It is like being a part of an exclusive club because as you learn the unwritten rules that others don't. YOU are on the "inside".

Whenever someone is on the inside that means there are outsiders. Everyone that is NOT in that group are considered "outsiders." When this thought process begins, the people in the group start to see others less as people with feelings and more as "not my people". It then becomes easier to be cruel, thoughtless, and exclusionary (meaning not including them with you or your group). This is how the Walnut Tree starts to take over the rest of the garden.

JOURNALING QUESTIONS

1. What surprised you most about your groups and unwritten rules in the activities you just completed?

_____

_____

_____

_____

_____

_____

_____

2. Are there groups that you have thought about leaving but just haven't done it? If so, what is stopping you from leaving?

As you come up with this answer keep adding to your answer until you get to a point where the worst case scenario could happen. Stop and look at the last answer... is that a reality? Is it something you could live with? Now go back and think about how often each of the things before the last one have happened to you – a little reality check.

_____

_____

_____

_____

_____

_____

_____

3. Were you surprised by your answers? After you went back and identified how many times those things have happened in the past, did it change your perspective at all? Why or why not?

_____

_____

_____

_____

_____

_____

_____

_____

_____

_____

_____

_____

_____

_____

_____

_____

_____

_____

CHAPTER 3
Growing Into A Marigold

WHAT IS A MARIGOLD?

The natural beauty of the marigold flower is easy to see; it brightens up any garden or flowerbed with a vibrant gold color and cheery petals. The beauty of the marigold is only half of it though. Marigolds produce a natural pesticide chemical from their roots, so strong it lasts years after they are gone, which in turn repels aphids and diseases. They are low maintenance, colorful, unique, and beautiful. However, marigolds are still susceptible to other insects and predators. They are not all-powerful, but make a great companion to certain other plants.

So, when you step back and look at this flower, it becomes clear that it is not only beautiful, but powerful, helpful, and generous. That being said, they are not super hero plants. They are still able to be hurt and require care to grow. These are many of the same qualities that describe a well rounded girl and woman as well. This is why the marigold was chosen for this book.

When describing a Marigold Girl, it is more than just being powerful, helpful and generous. These are all important elements, but really being a marigold girl involves finding ways to be authentic to yourself and your own values and beliefs, even when others around you are not. This sounds really easy to do in theory, but the reality of doing this during your teen years is one of the hardest things to do. It is a natural part of our human development to want to fit in with others and be part of a group. The challenge is to maintain your own values and beliefs while still finding ways to feel part of the groups you choose.

In his book, *Brainstorm*, Daniel Siegel describes this challenge in adolescence as something that is "basic survival" for teens as they become more independent from the adults around them. He explained that, at the core of this, "by being a part of an adolescent group, you get companionship on this transitional trek, as well as safety in numbers: predators will be intimidated by a large group, and you can lose yourself in the group mass." He went on to explain that "you can feel comforted in the group, strengthened by membership in the group, and even more creative in the creative intelligence of the group." Basically, he is saying that by being a part of a group in adolescence, you feel safe, more confident, and your creativity shines through. This is all true, until you don't!

When members of the group you have chosen begin to become aggressive (relational or otherwise) you can easily begin to lose your sense of self, and start becoming something you are not, in order to stay in the group and feel accepted. When looking at this from a biological viewpoint, it makes sense doesn't it? If you have different values and beliefs from the group, you risk standing alone and being alone during adolescence is one of the scariest thoughts. And now you know why it is so scary. It is something carried over in evolution; the need to belong as a form of survival. No wonder it is such a strong feeling and can cause us to make decisions that we wouldn't normally make!

Knowing this, gives you the power to see when it is happening in your life. There is power in understanding when people are making you feel uncomfortable or asking you to do things that you know, "in your gut", are against what you believe in. Your ability to step back and see things happening around you from an objective lens allows you to see what is happening without personalizing it. This makes it easier to make decisions that feel right to you and stay true to who you are today.

So what does it look like to live in Marigold Country? Here are a few ways to know you might be in that zone:

YOU ARE HAPPY TO SHARE EXPERIENCE, INFORMATION AND KNOWLEDGE WITH OTHERS.

You don't feel the need to compete all the time in your groups of friends. Many times, the reason behind this "lack of sharing of information" is because someone feels threatened that they will not know the most or be the best (or most popular). They think that by keeping all the information and knowledge to themselves, they have an advantage over others. Really the opposite is true, if the group shares what they know and experience, you will find that the information they have may begin to fit together like a puzzle and make everyone stronger and more confident.

WHEN WORKING TOGETHER YOU WORK EQUALLY AND SHARE THE REWARDS EQUALLY.

It's easy to want to be the one to take all the credit for something cool or exciting that happened, either with friends or in school. Many times you might see people who are trying to "edge others out" meaning, taking all the glory in a group and really not acknowledging the effort or experience of others. When you are with this person, how does it feel? If you are having trouble thinking of a time, think about this example.

In Science class, one of the assignments is to work together as a group to develop a science project. The teacher has allowed you to choose the people you want to work with and you were able to get two of your besties in your group. You work together to create an amazing project that is the hit of the science fair. When people come over to compliment you all on your work, one of your friends consistently steps forward and talks about all the work SHE did and how she came up with all the creative ideas. Whether or not your friend even knew she was doing this is beside the point, it still feels horrible.

Focusing on sharing the work and credit for the work with others is not always easy, especially when you have someone the group who is NOT participating in this process. So what can you do to help shift the focus in order to balance it and share the space?

First, try to find the talents of each person in the group on your own. Take a few minutes to talk with each of person or watch their actions. Play detective to see if you can find their strengths. Are they great at problem solving? Do they have a knack for writing or math? Maybe they are good negotiators during group conversations. Whatever it may be take a few of your own personal notes (mentally preferably) about each person, then help point them out during the group challenges that come up. Like this: "Samantha, I noticed that you were able to solve that crazy problem in math today. I was having a lot of trouble myself. Can you explain to me how you were able to see it?"

By identifying the strengths of people around you it naturally becomes a process for you to focus on the positive things. And let me tell you, positivity is contagious. This allows you to share other people's talents but also learn from them along the way. This benefits each person in the group because they are learning from others without even knowing it.

Secondly, try not to be greedy when accepting praise for tasks or results. What this means is to basically share the space and rewards (social rewards)with others. Think about this example:

Your good friend decides to run for class president. You and three of your friends jump right in to support her. You spend hours and hours creating posters, flyers, even come to school early and pass out buttons to everyone coming into school in the morning. Generally, you put your life on hold to help your friend achieve hers. And it works... SHE WINS! Teachers and parents are all talking to her about her accomplishment, mentioning how amazing the posters were and that they can't believe the creativity behind the flyers. She responds to them with a "thanks".

When she gives her acceptance speech, she talks all about the hard work she put in and how much she is looking forward to the job but she doesn't mention you or any of the other girls at all. On top of that, she starts spending more time with the "popular group" and less time with you.

What would your feelings be during this time? Usually, girls describe feeling betrayed, hurt, or angry in these situations. When you are able to stop and share the credit with the people around you it tends to stop (or at least slows) the social ladder climbing to the top. It also preserves relationships with people around you while still building new ones. This DOES NOT mean to disregard your effort or say things like, "Oh it totally wasn't even me, Jane did all the work on this." There is a way to receive the compliment and share that other people were also contributors. Try: "Thanks so much, it was a lot of hard work and we could not have done it without Jane's artwork on those posters."

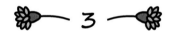

3

YOU ENJOY WATCHING OTHERS GROW AND FLOURISH AND TEND TO NOT SEE THINGS AS A COMPETITION AS MUCH AS A CHANCE TO LEARN AND GROW.

This one takes a bit of practice because when we see others doing better than us our first instinct tends to be to compare ourselves to them and their accomplishments. Even as adults, we fight this urge constantly. When you are working on this skill consider asking yourself these questions:

What can I learn from this person's success?
How did they do it?
What can I add to my information bank for next time?
What did they do differently that I might be able to try?

If you don't know the answer to these...ask them! Remember that each time you learn from another person's success, you grow as well. If you start to find yourself frustrated or jealous, STOP, take a breath and remind yourself that your time is coming too. I guarantee that there is someone somewhere in your life that is looking at you and thinking about how they wish they could do the things you do. There is something in YOU that speaks to someone else and can also teach them about YOUR success.

Sometimes these things might not be easy to see in yourself, so, if you are having trouble seeing the successes you have had recently, ask someone close to you (a teacher or trusted adult). Many times, they can give you objective feedback on the small and big successes you have had. Think about asking them one or more of these questions:

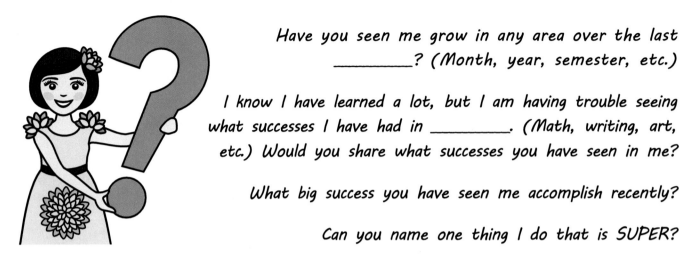

Have you seen me grow in any area over the last _____? (Month, year, semester, etc.)

I know I have learned a lot, but I am having trouble seeing what successes I have had in _____. (Math, writing, art, etc.) Would you share what successes you have seen in me?

What big success you have seen me accomplish recently?

Can you name one thing I do that is SUPER?

Before you roll you eyes and say, "There is no way I can do that!" let me stop you. As girls and women, we often have trouble accepting compliments or asking for someone to help us see the positive qualities in ourselves (more on that later). For now, know this...when you uncover the magic of embracing the positive things others see in you, you gain both power and confidence. It takes practice and you have to stop that voice in your head that wants to fight what it (instead saying negative things) but, when you strengthen this muscle of acceptance you become a stronger person that is able to accomplish more than you ever imagined. Just try it for a month, use the journals in this book to make notes about your experience, then re-read it. My guess is that you will surprise yourself!

✿— 4 —✿
YOU TEND TO HAVE A GROWTH MINDSET

If you haven't heard of growth mindset yet, you will probably be exposed to it in one of your classes soon. This concept was developed by Carol Dweck, PhD, and she defined it as this: "In a growth mindset, people believe that their most basic abilities can be developed through dedication and hard work – brains and talent are just the starting point. This view creates a love of learning and a resilience that is essential for great accomplishment." If you are not in a growth mindset, you are living in a FIXED mindset where you think you "can't do things" because you just don't have the ability. In the GROWTH mindset, your perspective changes and you see yourself as constantly growing, learning new things by failing and learning from your mistakes. This "F word" is a good thing! FAILURE is a growth opportunity. Instead of obstacles, you see challenges!

The theory has proven that with work and perseverance, people tend to learn more and learn it more quickly. Skills (and attitudes about your skills) are improved when you are able to view challenges and failures as opportunities instead of a reflection on how smart or capable you are. Changing your thoughts can change your whole perspective. What you think you believe and what you believe you become! When we are constantly having negative thoughts and doubting ourselves, we start to believe that we are that negative person. It is an easy hole to fall into, but with practice you can change and strengthen that mindset.

YOU ARE ABLE TO TAKE CRITICISM AND COMPLIMENTS IN ORDER TO GROW FROM THEM

The two big C's are, often times, the hardest thing for girls and women to manage. I specify girls and women because historically, men do not appear to have as much difficulty with criticism and compliments. Here are some ways to manage compliments:

Stop responding to a compliment with a put down about yourself!

If you friend tells you that they think you look great that day, don't feel the need to immediately respond with a negative tagged onto the end like, "Ugh, I feel so fat, but thanks".

Do the same for a friend!

If you hear a friend respond with a putdown after you give her a compliment, stop and reinforce that you really meant it. Perhaps you are walking down the hall and someone says to her, "I love your haircut, Jane!" and she responds with "Aww thanks, but I think it looks so bad on me. I didn't want it this short." Take a moment and just say something like, "I think it looks great and it sounds like Samantha did too".

Don't be afraid to compliment yourself!

If you studied hard for a test and aced it, you should be able to say, "I am so proud of myself for getting an A on that test. It was hard!"

If a friend compliments you, take their word and believe it!

Think about this. Do you give someone a compliment if you don't want to or don't mean it? Usually the answer to this is no. When someone takes the time to notice something great about another person and then tells them, you can probably believe that they mean it. So the next time someone gives you a compliment, remember that they saw something in you that made them stop and tell you!

Find something you are proud of every day and remind yourself of it!

It is easy to get distracted by all the negative things that happen around us all day. However, when all you focus on is the negative, it starts to become the way you think in general. Remember before when you read that positivity is contagious? This is not only true with others but with yourself as well. There is a whole theory in psychology built around this called Positive Psychology. So even if you have to set a reminder for yourself on your calendar 3-4 times per day, DO IT. Stop and take a moment to think of something positive that happened, or something you have been grateful for during the day.

If a negative thought pops into your head, replace it with the opposite!

Like many of the other things you have read, this takes practice. If your "go to" thought is a negative one when you approach something hard or someone gives you a compliment, then you have to strengthen that positive response muscle. At first, you might need other people around you to remind you to do it (this could be a trusted adult or another girl who is working on the same skill). Eventually, you will begin to recognize it yourself, and when that happens, you are just steps away from moving to a positive mindset. So when a negative thought pops in like, "I suck at math", stop and turn it into, "I made it half way through that test this time." or "Man, that was hard, but I tried my best and I will work on those I missed so I can get them next time."

Say "THANK YOU" when you receive a compliment and resist saying more!

Again...this is hard one but it will do wonders to change your thoughts about yourself. At first, you might find yourself starting to add the negative statement behind your thank you but it is ok to stop mid sentence when you recognize yourself doing it and just say, "You know what? Thank you." Two simple words show the person giving you the compliment that you value yourself as well as them.

YOU ARE INCLUSIVE OF PEOPLE BUT NOT WALKED ALL OVER

Welcoming others into a group is not always easy and, quite frankly, not always necessary. Let me clarify. Being inclusive does not mean that you have to include everyone in everything you do with all your friends. What it DOES Mean is that you use empathy with others to take their feelings into consideration and include them when possible and appropriate.

Let's say you were a party of a group of girls who usually sit together during lunch in a particular spot on campus. You eat there every day with the same group of girls. One day a girl you know from math class comes over and asks to sit with you guys. She isn't someone who normally hangs out with you and you really only know her from class discussions. Being inclusive means that you welcome her to eat lunch with you but that doesn't mean you have to add her to your text group or schedule a time to hang out. It also doesn't mean that you "allow her" to sit with you but really don't talk to her.

Inclusive means you use the time with her to get to know her. You can ask questions and see what you might have in common. You may find that you don't have much in common at all and it may not blossom into any kind of stronger friendship, but, and this is a BIG but, you have honored her as a person and showed genuine interest and respect for her. This is a key factor in being a Marigold Girl.

On the flip side of this is when you honor and respect someone and they don't show the same to you in return. Let's say that the same scenario occurs expect this time, the girl enters and immediately hits it off with another one of the girls in your group but you don't really feel the same connection. The "new girl" makes some statements that just don't make you feel good.

 *When something like this happens, you have every right to stand up for yourself. Being inclusive does NOT mean accepting abuse or getting "walked over" by other people. When someone is being disrespectful to you, it is 100% okay to tell them that you don't appreciate it and maybe even remove yourself from the situation. It may feel a bit uncomfortable to do it, but you send a clear message that you are respectful and will give it to others that engage in MUTUAL respect.*

So after all this you may be asking, why even choose to be a Marigold? After all, this all sounds like a lot of work right? The short answer is "yes", it is work. However, the great thing about Marigold Girls is that through this work, each one of you is able to achieve an understanding of how others around you interact so that it makes a little more sense and ultimately makes your life a little easier to manage.

Really, being a Marigold Girl is a two part process. The first is really just gaining some new information about how the social language, and interactions, of girls works and why some girls act and say the things that they do. This alone is a powerful piece of information that helps you put things in perspective when they may start to feel a little "crazy" in your social circle.

The second part is the true gift that you give yourself and the people around you. When you choose to use the information you have learned (by modeling and teaching through example) it makes you more confident and powerful. Like any other skill that you teach others, the reward is not in the praise you receive, but in the feeling you have when you see others also make changes. Along the way you will run into challenges and pitfalls but this is a normal part of learning any skill. Working to be authentic to yourself and understand and manage the social language of others, especially girls, is a tough skill to master. Just a reminder to be gentle with yourself.

Growing into a Marigold is a process and being able to do all the things listed above is not something that happens overnight. Find ways to incorporate some of these things when you can and you will find that you will evolve into using them regularly. As each of the things you try become natural parts of you, it is easier to add another, until you have a tool belt full of ways to stand tall as your own person.

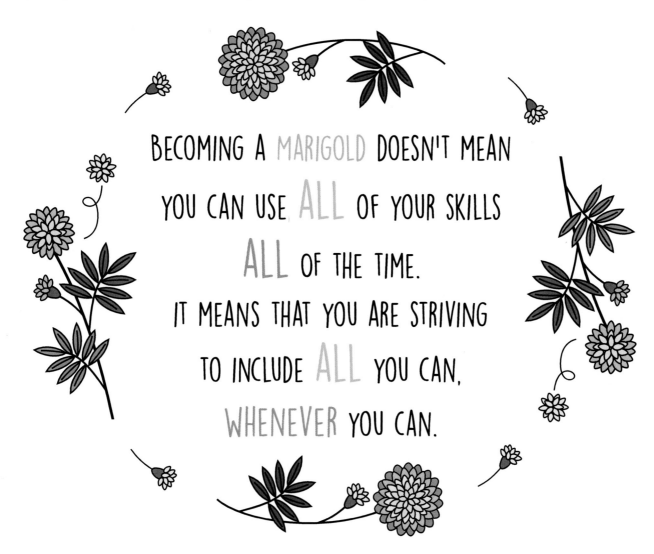

BECOMING A MARIGOLD DOESN'T MEAN YOU CAN USE ALL OF YOUR SKILLS ALL OF THE TIME. IT MEANS THAT YOU ARE STRIVING TO INCLUDE ALL YOU CAN, WHENEVER YOU CAN.

If you are not there yet, then find yourself a Marigold around you and hang out with her whenever you can. You will find that her positive attitude, encouragement and support will be contagious and become part of you as well. You will begin to thrive by being around another Marigold, which will help you grow into your own.

ACTIVITIES

1. Take the challenge of asking a trusted adult or teacher about your successes by interviewing them with one or more of the following questions:

1. Have you seen me grow in any area over the last... (month, year, semester)? How?

_____

_____

_____

_____

2. I know I have learned a lot but I am having trouble seeing what successes I have had in (math, writing, art, etc). Would you share what successes you have seen in me?

_____

_____

_____

_____

3. What was the biggest success you have seen me accomplish recently?

_____

_____

_____

_____

4. Can you name one thing that I do that is SUPER?

_____

_____

2. For one week, log each compliment you receive in the Compliment Tracker on the following page. Make sure to not only include what they said but what you initially thought and then how you responded.

3. At the end of the week review the results:

Did the results surprise you? If yes, how?

_____

_____

_____

_____

_____

_____

Can you see patterns of certain people that might be more complimentary than others in your world? How can you use this information to create a more positive, supportive space for yourself?

_____

_____

_____

_____

_____

_____

_____

_____

_____

# MY COMPLIMENT TRACKER

DATE	FROM	COMPLIMENT	INITIAL THOUGHTS	MY RESPONSE

JOURNALING QUESTIONS

1. When was the last time you received a compliment from someone? How did it make you feel?

_____

_____

_____

_____

2. What was your first reaction when they gave it to you?

_____

_____

_____

_____

3. What is one negative thought that keeps entering your head that you can't seem to change?

_____

_____

_____

4. How could you replace that phrase with an opposite phrase that uses a growth mindset?

_____

_____

_____

CHAPTER 4
Dealing With The Walnut Tree

Let's talk about the walnut tree. The walnut tree gives off a toxin called Juglone from its roots, which slows or stops some plants' growth. This gradually makes most everything under the walnut tree wilt, and ultimately die. It is a beautiful tree that supplies walnuts, but it is selfish. When we are talking about this with relational aggression you can think of this poison as a couple of different things that may come up in your life. Specifically, comparison and jealousy.

It may feel like a win if you are "at the top," but ask most girls at the top and they will tell you that it takes A LOT of effort to try to stay there. This crazy roller coaster that your teen brain has you on kind of holds you hostage to how others see you. You can tell yourself all day that you don't care, but the physical changes in the make up of your brain will override you. The desire for acceptance from your friends and others around you dominates any other rational part of your brain that is trying to hang on. This is part of the reason why social media is such a challenge. When you post a picture, have you ever stopped to ask yourself, "What is the *goal* of posting this picture?" Is it to educate others and enlighten them about the composition of your photo? Usually NOT; the goal is to see how many people will like it.

Why? Because your brain is actually craving it! Our body produces a chemical called Dopamine. Dopamine is the main brain chemical that is responsible for that feeling of "reward" you get when you are feeling good about something. With each "Like" you get, each positive comment you receive, you have a virtual slot machine of this "feel good" chemical paying out in your brain. So it makes sense that people will do anything they can to keep this feeling going. However, when you see other people's posts, the first thoughts that go through your head usually involve how you add up to them.

You start comparing yourself to them, and this might even happen without your knowing you are doing it. This is the danger zone...this is where the poison from the tree starts to invade your flower soil. It eats away at your self-esteem and self-confidence slowly until you have difficulty recognizing any positive things about yourself after awhile. Walnut Tree Girls tend to capitalize on this and will often find ways to use comparison that make themselves look the best OR even to make their "target" look bad.

A girl that falls into this category can be tricky to spot at first because they can be very charming and friendly. Just like the walnut tree, they hide their toxicity and release it slowly, often making it hard to see or recognize. What does this look like? Well, be on the lookout for some of the following signs.

SIGNS OF THE WALNUT TREE GIRL

 They may appear supportive and happy, acting as a close friend to you, but as you observe and watch with your investigative eye, you might see signs of manipulation and selfishness.

 They may tend to be negative and take credit for ideas, whether or not the ideas are their own, perhaps taking credit for what you or another did, attempting to include you afterward.

 They are constantly competing with others, usually revolving around getting attention.

 They have difficulty sharing the space and often only want to help you when it is also benefits themselves in some way.

 They may complain about other people gossiping, but they really just want to be the one to start the rumor. By starting the rumor, they have control over what is being spread.

 You may see or hear them say something negative about you but when you confront them they use the excuse that they were "just kidding" or even outright lie that they said it. They may throw you under the bus with friends in a conversation and then tell you later that they didn't mean to do that at all.

 You may even hear them say bad things about someone then when they see them in person they couldn't be nicer to them.

Whatever the case, you will know you are around a Walnut Tree Girl when you start to begin to feel insecure, depressed, discouraged, embarrassed, or bad about yourself when you are near her. You may start to doubt your own ideas and beliefs about things. Initially you may defend these ideas or thoughts to her but you start to find that you are wilting and it gets harder to defend because it continues regardless of your efforts. This is your first sign to go find a Marigold!

THE PROGRESSION OF THE POISON

Though not every situation follows a clear path, as you start to recognize the elements of a walnut tree in others you will begin to see a progression (path) that their behavior follows. It tends to begin with teasing, then moves to isolation from other friends and people, followed by degradation (which is a fancy word for making you feel bad about yourself), and ending with domination, where the Walnut Tree Girl can easily control and manipulate yo

Teasing ⤳ *Degradation* ⤳ *Isolation* ⤳ *Domination*

UGH! Even as I write this it sounds overwhelming, so let's break this down a bit to look at how we might be able to recognize each stop on this path.

❀ — Teasing — ❀

Teasing is not always a bad thing. It is something that happens between friends and family and friendly teasing (truly joking) WITH someone else is a healthy part of a relationship. It is usually done with someone that knows you so well that they know what your boundaries are within the relationship. They know what kind of teasing or joke would be hurtful and stop at that line. This positive form of teasing helps you form bonds and create inside jokes with friends, which creates stronger relationships.

So when does it become negative? Teasing can move to relational aggressive behavior when it is meant to intentionally hurt you or someone else. The tricky part is that often times it moves from the positive kind of teasing to the negative kind with someone who knows you well.

You may have had a wonderful friendship with them and could tease each other together then you notice that she begins to use some of these inside jokes or other teasing comments to start embarrassing you or making you feel bad. Most of the time it is followed up with a "just kidding" or "I'm only joking" comment.

When this starts to happen, it can feel really confusing. Pay attention to your feelings and honor them. If this is a friend with history, tell them how you feel and see if they acknowledge and make change. If they apologize and don't change the behavior, it may be a warning sign that they are moving away from your circle.

1

Misty and Monica met in Kindergarten, and from the first day of school they were fast friends. They had play dates and were stuck together like glue. As they grew up, their friendship continued with sleep overs and their families even spent a few holiday breaks vacationing together. On one vacation, they played truth or dare and during one of the dares Misty snorted milk out of her nose so hard that it caused them both to fall off their chairs laughing hysterically. They both laughed so hard that Monica peed her pants a little. After this vacation every time they made each other crack up, one of them ended up saying that was a "pee milker"! (Corny, I know, but they thought it was *HILLLAAARRRIOUS!*)

2

When they entered middle school new relationships started to form for each girl and Monica noticed that Misty was starting to hang out with the "cool kids" more and more. As she gained status in the group, Monica felt her friendship start to slip away. They didn't see each other as much and when they did it was sometimes awkward. One day a break in the awkwardness found its place and Monica and Misty were both having lunch with the cool kids. Someone told a joke that made them all burst out laughing. Monica was laughing so hard that she almost couldn't catch her breath, and just then Misty turned to Monica and said laughingly, "Don't pee your pants Monica! You know I'm kidding, girl."

Here is an example of both types of teasing. First, it was a healthy bonding form where both girls felt like they had created a moment of a sacred inside joke that bonded them together with an experience that only they understood. So when "pee milker" was said, they both knew it was a reference to a fun time they experienced together...laughing WITH each other. In the second part of the example, Misty used the inside information to embarrass Monica. Even if the rest of the group did not know the whole story, it was a violation of the trust in the friendship and used to knock Monica down in the group's status, with Misty laughing AT her.

Now here is the kicker. More than likely, Misty did not even realize why she did it or even how much it impacted Monica. She did it because it was an "in the moment" chance to climb a step up the ladder in the "cool group".

Degradation

Teasing is a first stage because it opens the door for someone to use words to make you feel bad. The next stage is degradation. Degradation means to lower your self esteem or rank socially. The definition of degradation in the Merriam-Webster Dictionary is, "To lower in dignity or estimation" or "To reduce (someone) to a lower rank or degree." So, when you think about this stage, think about it as someone trying to use words and actions to lower your self confidence and self esteem while also finding ways to start moving you out of any popular circles you may have been a part of (or are trying to be part of).

Let's use Misty and Monica again as we move into these next levels. Monica didn't want to give up on her friendship with Misty because...well...they had been friends forever and Monica felt like if she only hung in there and tried just a little harder she might be able to find her "old Misty" eventually. She continued to hang out with Misty even though she was realizing that she was starting to not feel so great around her a lot of the time. Misty continued to say things that were "teasing" but really it felt like she was saying things to make other people laugh at Monica.

Plus, Misty would always follow it up with an "I'm sorry" or say things like "you know I'm kidding right?" or "Don't be so sensitive Monica, it was only a joke". Despite these types of comments, Misty was still included in the "cool group" and was usually invited to hang out or to parties with Misty and the other kids in the group. However, recently, Misty started to say and do things that were extra embarrassing, like comment on Monica's new haircut with an eye roll and say things like, "you're still playing with slime?" Followed by laughter and a hair toss. Of course this would make the other girls in the group laugh along with her and Monica was starting to feel like she couldn't really find a way to connect with many of them, especially Misty.

Isolation

With isolation, it starts to become difficult to know where you belong. At this stage you might start to feel really left out of circles and activities that you have felt really comfortable in previously. People that had been friends, especially the Walnut Tree Girl, begin to leave you out and you feel isolated from your social circles, finding yourself alone (or at least it feels that way). Here is the thing about this stage though. You are NOT alone!

The problem is that when we begin to feel left out of familiar circles, without an understanding of why, we tend to get tunnel vision. We want so badly to understand why we are being left out, and find ways to work our way back into the familiar group, that we cannot see other opportunities for friendship around us. If you are able to realize that you are in this stage and can take a step back, you will begin to gain perspective and notice so many other social opportunities that you can jump into. That being said, it does NOT feel good to walk away from the familiar, even when it feels bad to be in it. BUT, if you continue to get stuck in the Walnut Tree Girl's path you will eventually start to feel desperate for approval and acceptance.

This is when it moves to the last stage of isolation. In Misty and Monica's case, Monica had been dealing with Misty (and other girls) "teasing" her and degrading her for months. Monica was part of a few outside sports teams and a theater group, but when she had any free time she chose to try to make it to ANY activity Misty would invite her too. Mostly because Misty was starting to limit her invitations.

Monica would really only be invited to parties or events where Misty needed help or asked her to bring something. It was very rare that she spent any really individual or friend-time with Misty anymore and when they did, it was all talk about Misty. They didn't share many inside jokes anymore, partially because Misty thought it was lame but also because Monica started to feel fearful of sharing anything with her since Misty often used it against her. Most of the time at school, Monica would eat lunch with Misty and the "cool kids" but she always found herself sitting on the outside of the circle, not really feeling included and obviously not invited *into* the circle either.

Domination

When a relationship enters this final stage, usually you start to feel beat down and alone. When this happens you may find yourself saying or doing things you normally wouldn't. You may not feel comfortable doing or saying these things, but you do them anyway at the request of your Walnut Tree Girl and/or the friends in that circle. This isn't because you are a bad person or regularly make bad decisions. Instead, you might be doing things that make you feel bad about your self in order to sustain status or fit in or keep the friendship. They can be small things (like agreeing when you don't really agree in a conversation) to big things (like illegal activity). At this stage, the Walnut Tree has officially taken over the garden and you no longer are standing in your own truth. When it gets to this level, you are not your authentic self. Instead, you are a version of the Walnut Tree.

Monica had been dealing with the isolation and negative comments for months now and although she really felt bad about herself she continued to try to save her friendship through savoring the small moments that she feel "the old Misty". These moments were few and far between, but every once in awhile...she felt it. She knew her old friend was in there somewhere. Misty had invited Monica to a few more parties and activities outside of school and Monica heard that their old friend, Sarah from elementary school, moved back into town from Europe (her family was in the military stationed there for a couple of years) Monica was thrilled! She couldn't wait for their old friend to join the group again, but the joy was short-lived.

Monica went to lunch as usual with the group, and on their way to sit down, Monica said, "Guess what, Misty, you will never believe it, but Sarah is back in town. Her family moved back and she is starting here at school with us next week". Misty gave an epic eye-roll and said, "Oh geez...not *Sarah*. She is such a pain in the ass. Don't you remember how *lame* she was, Monica?" Monica stopped for a moment and even though she wanted to argue back, she felt the eyes of the other five girls staring her down and all that came out was, "Yeah." Over the next couple of weeks, Sarah tried multiple times to join the group and reconnect with Monica, but each time, Misty would pull her away or tell Monica to ignore Sarah. Monica felt HORRIBLE, but she knew if she didn't, she would lose her friendship with Misty completely. There was something that kept her there and something that kept her from speaking her truth, and she felt trapped. She was DOMINATED by the situation and her friend.

TENDING YOUR GARDEN AND FINDING SUPPORT

Walnut trees are part of the garden but so are you and others around you. By focusing on strengthening your own marigold and the other marigolds around you, the walnut tree can be stopped in its tracks. So there is no need to chop it down! In other words there is no need to turn the tables when relational aggression is happening. In many movies you see the heroine combat the girl bullies with the same aggression they have suffered. My point here is that this tactic only spreads the poison and infects your marigolds. That doesn't mean you should not stand up for yourself, it only means that you can use other ways of advocating for yourself. Ways that don't involve treating others the same negative way. If you can focus on the positive and finding ways to live at a higher level, the Walnut Tree Girl has no power over you and cannot poison your soil or take over your flower garden. In no way am I saying you should take the abuse. *Let me say that again:*

YOU SHOULD NEVER FEEL THAT YOU NEED TO ACCEPT ABUSIVE BEHAVIOR FROM OTHERS. WHEN SOMEONE IS BULLYING YOU OR MAKING YOU FEEL BAD, IT IS YOUR RIGHT TO STAND UP FOR YOURSELF AND ADVOCATE FOR YOUR OWN SAFETY, BOTH PHYSICALLY AND EMOTIONALLY.

What I *am* saying is that using tools to shift your perspective allows you to make choices about how you respond in situations. Instead of just reacting out of fear, you may begin to find that the changes in the way you respond lead to a more powerful sense of self, ultimately feeling happier and stronger.

Walnut Tree Girls may be difficult, but it is important to remember that the root causes for the way they act are not because they are evil people (even though it may feel that way sometimes). A Walnut Tree Girl functions this way out of FEAR. Fear of losing her group, fear of losing status, or fear of being alone. Fear is the driving source of all Walnut Trees even though they may not admit it or even know it. So when you run across one, you might take some time to see what they are afraid of. Use their words and actions as clues to solve the mystery. After awhile you will start to see patterns of their behavior that lead you back to what they might be afraid of and once you are able to see it, you may see the Walnut Tree Girl from a different perspective.

ACTIVITIES

1. Interview a woman in your life that you trust asking any or all of the following questions:

1. When you were my age was there someone that made you feel bad about yourself in your circle of friends? What did they do?

_____

_____

_____

2. Do you remember a time when a friend turned on you or did something that made you question whether or not they were a good friend? What happened? How did you handle it?

_____

_____

_____

3. Did you have someone in school that everyone knew was the "mean girl" or "bully"? Why did people think that? What did you think of her?

_____

_____

_____

4. Did you ever do anything mean to other girls or even friends to try to fit into a group or be popular when you were in school?

_____

_____

_____

2. In this activity, it will be easy to see who has the most positive influence on you and your feelings about yourself as you look at the list objectively.

1. List the girls that surround your life by writing a name in each circle.
2. Underneath each name write 3 adjectives that describe how you feel when you are around her. Try not to over think it - write the first thing that comes to mind.
3. Highlight or circle the positive adjectives.

NAME: _____
1. _____
2. _____
3. _____

NAME: _____
1. _____
2. _____
3. _____

NAME: _____
1. _____
2. _____
3. _____

ME

NAME: _____
1. _____
2. _____
3. _____

NAME: _____
1. _____
2. _____
3. _____

NAME: _____
1. _____
2. _____
3. _____

JOURNALING QUESTIONS

1. Did the list of girls you made surprise you? Why or why not?

_____

_____

_____

_____

_____

_____

_____

_____

_____

2. Is there someone in your life that you think might be a walnut tree girl? What kind of things that she does make you think that?

_____

_____

_____

_____

_____

_____

_____

CHAPTER 5

Daffodils and Snowdrops, Daisies and Weeds

In a garden there is usually more than one or two types of plants and trees. Just like in life, there will be more than just one challenging person to understand and deal with. We have talked quite a bit about the hardiness of marigolds and their ability to avoid the poison of the walnut tree, but did you know there are other flowers that have similar abilities?

They all have varying tolerances of the poison given off by the walnut tree but the snowdrop and the daffodil are also one of a number of flowers that are able to grow in the same vicinity of the walnut tree. When thinking about this as our metaphor for friendships, I think it is easy to see how we may have others around us that don't necessarily share all our same qualities but can still be supports and positive influences. This may be friends, but it may also be supportive adults, family or community relationships. Looking for those Daffodils and Snowdrops are ways to increase your circle, and in this you may find more Marigolds (people you connect with who are authentic to themselves).

So what about the Daisies and Weeds you ask? Well, these are the girls who hang with the Walnut Tree Girl but are not true to their authentic selves. The daisies are beautiful flowers and have wonderful qualities but when they are planted around a walnut tree the poison slowly starts to take over and they eventually wilt and die. Obviously, the girls will not die, but wilting is a real possibility. When we are not able to be authentic and true to who we really are (and want to be) we wilt inside by putting on a mask or face for others. So in a metaphoric way, their true self is wilting.

Now let's take a minute to talk about weeds. What is the first thought that comes up for you? How would you describe them? My bet is you said something to the effect of annoying, can't get rid of them, they are everywhere, invade every nook and cranny. Well, maybe not the last one (that's kind of old-person lingo), but the basis of weed is that they are in others' business and it's hard to get rid of them. When we relate this to the "popular group", the weeds will be the person or people that always seem to be in everyone else's business. These are the girls who make sure they know all the juicy gossip and then relay it to the Walnut Tree Girl. By taking on this role, they are attempting to secure a space for themselves next to the leader of the group. If she can provide information than she is valuable right? At least, that is the theory. Also, if she is making sure the focus is always on other people, than there is less of a chance that the focus will be on HER! She is often described as "two-faced" and the group knows that you don't tell her secrets and try not to talk about anything around her that you don't want "everyone" to know.

Interestingly enough, the actions of the Weed have similar roots to the Walnut Tree Girl. She is functioning out of fear, but for her it is usually fear that she will be discarded or thrown out of the group if she can't prove herself to be worthy with the information she gives. Many times this arises from a girl who has moved through teasing and degradation, but before she is isolated from the group she starts to realize that if she gets a jump on the Walnut Tree and is able to provide information and do what she thinks the Walnut Tree wants, she will secure a space in the group. Often, it works. Not because she is liked or respected for it, but because she has now made it clear that she can be dominated.

Imagine the situation with Misty and Monica again, except this time, imagine that when Misty started to degrade Monica with negative and embarrassing comments. Monica decided to start deflecting the conversations by sharing gossip she had heard about other girls. This shifted conversations and people started to LISTEN to Monica. She now started to feel like she was actually a part of the group and people were paying attention to her and valuing her contributions. At least, that is how it felt initially, until she began to experience the backlash from the people she had been gossiping about. She started to slowly lose friends outside of the "cool group" as people didn't trust her anymore. People got quiet when she was around and often she got dirty looks from other people at school. For awhile she told herself it didn't matter because she was part of Misty's group. However, as time went on, she started to find that in order to keep her status in the "popular group" she had to keep providing new and juicier information, which was hard to do. She found herself starting to exaggerate stories, even lying a couple of times. This not only caused more problems with other girls outside of the group but she started to feel even worse about herself than she did before.

The take away from this chapter is simple. Pay attention to those around you. If you see Weeds invading your territory, take a stand and politely ask for your privacy. You are not being rude if you are in a personal conversation with another person. You could also just shift the conversation to something neutral like the weather or sports then shift back once she leaves.

I would even argue that politely calling them out on their behavior could be beneficial. One might say something like, "I really don't want to share with you because I am afraid you are not going to be able to keep it between us". This sets a boundary and lets the girl know that you are aware of her behavior without verbally assaulting her or being rude. You are kind, but assertive.

And, as far as the Daffodils and Snowdrops, just look around you. You might be surprised to find a different set of people that you didn't expect to be your supports, that might even lead you to more Marigolds.

ACTIVITY

Draw your garden!

1. Start on this page by listing all the elements in your garden; the walnut tree, marigolds, snowdrops, daffodils, daisies and weeds.
2. Pair names of the people in your circle with the elements. Include yourself!
3. Turn to the next page and draw the elements anywhere you want in your garden. Make it as simple or intricate as you would like.
4. When you are finished, answer the journaling questions about your drawing.

GARDEN ELEMENT	NAME OF PERSON
	ME!

My Garden!

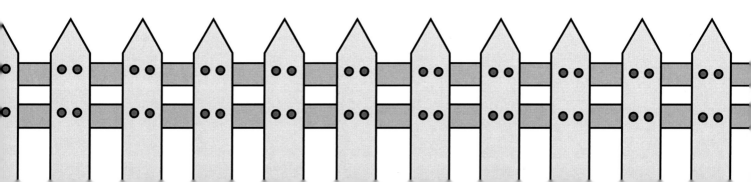

CLIP THIS PAGE OUT AND PUT IT
SOMEWHERE YOU'LL SEE OFTEN!

JOURNALING QUESTIONS

1. Were you surprised at all by your drawing? Why or why not?

_____

_____

_____

2. Are there snowdrop and daffodil people in your life that might be supports that you have not recognized? Why or why not?

_____

_____

_____

3. How many Marigold Girls do you have in your garden? Do you hang out with them in or out of school? If not, what is stopping you?

_____

_____

_____

4. Based on where you placed each of the elements, ask yourself:

Are your marigolds all close together or spread apart?

_____

Is your walnut tree GIANT or small and growing?

_____

How many snowdrops and daffodils are in your drawing?

_____

Where are they in relation to you in the garden?

_____

Do you have weeds? A lot or a little? Are they invading the whole garden, or focused on just one or a few elements of it?

_____

Where are your daisies? Do you think any of these might turn into marigolds at some point?

_____

5. What are a few things you learned about yourself?

_____

_____

_____

_____

_____

_____

_____

CHAPTER 6

Hold On! We All Have A Bit Of EACH In Us!

As you start dissecting what roles everyone is playing in your life around you, let's consider one big thing. We all have pieces of each of these in who we are. We can all be Walnut Trees, Marigolds and even Weeds at different points in our days, weeks, months, or years within our life. So as you begin to think about all of this information, please do not label people with permanent marker! I have seen many girls be all of these things at different points in their lives and they were all amazing human beings. The goal is to try to achieve Marigold status as much as possible in your life, and if you find that someone around you is wilting your bouquet, continue on your way and be their Marigold when you can. Just know that everyone can change and grow, and one day they may join (or re-join) your bunch.

I went back and forth debating whether or not to write a *personal* account about this for you, but in order to drive this point home I decided to set aside my humiliation and give you this example. So, here it goes…

PART 1 – FALLING VICTIM TO THE WALNUT TREE GIRLS

My family moved around a lot when I was a young girl. When I was about 9 years old, we landed in a town where my parents put me in a private school that was really small, and most of the kids had been there together since Kindergarten. We had about fifteen kids in our classes. I spent 6th grade through 8th grade there, and MAN were there some Walnut Trees!

I was a pretty shy girl, but I learned from all our moves how to fit in with a variety of different people. I was kind of like a chameleon in most occasions, where I learned to read a room and see what people liked and didn't like pretty quickly so I was able to adapt and have conversations. The downside of this was that I was rarely myself because I was so busy trying to "fit in". This kind of social superpower grew as I got older, because as you enter middle school you have to really be a chameleon to fit in with the "popular kids", and by high school I was a pro.

So, back to middle school. There was a clique of three girls that ruled our class. I thought I was playing the game pretty well and fitting in with them, but they would often make comments about my clothes or other things that hurt my feelings. They would immediately say something like, "Whatever, don't be so sensitive!" and I thought I might have misunderstood. I distinctly remember one day of mean girl behavior that has stuck with me. I had shorts on because it was hot outside, and they all came to sit next to me. I thought maybe they were going to invite me to eat with them at lunch or do something after school, but instead, the worst happened.

They all started pointing at my legs and laughing. "Oh my God! Look at her legs! They are so HAIRY!", one said. The others giggled and continued with, "I can't believe you don't even shave your legs yet. You are so gross." I wanted to DIE! I went home and cried, and immediately shaved my legs.

This was the beginning of my journey with relational aggression (mean girls). But here is the thing. In this case, I was a victim of the Walnut Tree, but there are multiple parts to this story, just as there are multiple parts to us as human beings.

PART 2 – INTRODUCING... THE WALNUT TREE GIRL IN ME

This is where I humble myself to say that over the next few years I survived other occasions of mean girl incidents, although, at the time I don't think I really knew that's what they were. I just knew they made me feel bad and I had to do whatever I could to get out of these situations. So, as I entered high school, I found myself maneuvering around friendships to find the ones that fit me the best but could ALSO provide me that all-wanting popularity that comes with being in high school. I struggled a lot with finding that balance, like I now know many girls did, but on one occasion in particular I failed miserably.

There was a new girl who came to the school from out of town. She was beautiful, and of course, all the boys wanted to date her and all the girls wanted to be her friend. Well, she tended to be a bit of a Walnut Tree in that she enjoyed the attention and really sought it out in some not-so-subtle ways from the boys. At the time, my boyfriend was one of the boys swooning over her. Let's just say, she did not stop him from doing so, and I pretty much lost it.

So in a very NON-Marigold way, I went out one night with a friend and "borrowed" a flashing open trench sign, placed it on the new girl's front lawn, and proceeded to add a "little" toilet paper to her trees. Even as I write this I am embarrassed and mortified that I could have participated in this! At least I didn't get away with it. The next morning, the police hunted me down at my girlfriend's house (I was sleeping over) and told me that I had to go apologize or I might find myself with a criminal record. I did just that — I was scared straight!

In the scope of things, I was not a person who had consistent toxic friendships, but it was definitely a mean thing to do and aligned completely with the elements of a Walnut Tree.

The point of this story is that we all have multiple parts to who we are, especially as we move into our teenage years. As we start to navigate our way through the social landscape of being a teen there are a lot of bumps in the road. You will not always be a Marigold, BUT, you will also not always be a Walnut Tree. This is something to remember about others around you too!

THE KEY TO ACHIEVING MARIGOLD STATUS IS NOT TO ALWAYS BE PERFECT.

IT IS TO...

ADMIT WHEN YOU ARE NOT PERFECT.
RESOLVE ANY HARM CAUSED.
FORGIVE YOURSELF.
LEARN FROM THE EXPERIENCE.

Each of the experiences you have as elements in your garden will shape your perspective and give you empathy for others in the future. I'll be honest…ages 10-18 are pretty brutal, and even a few years beyond that as you find yourself in search of who you really are and want to be. This is completely normal! As long as you are aware of your actions you can make better choices.

As famous poet and author, Maya Angelou, said, "Do the best you can until you know better. Then when you know better, *do* better."

ACTIVITY

Take some time to reflect over the roles of Marigold, Walnut Tree or Weed you may have played recently.

On the following page you will find a chart.
Write down what you have done or said that would fall into each of the categories.

BE HONEST!

After you are done, review which column has the most listed.

ARE YOU A MARIGOLD MOST OF THE TIME?

Congratulations! Keep up the good work and try to keep that column long!

ARE YOU A WEED OR A WALNUT TREE MOST OF THE TIME?
DO NOT FRET!

All this means is that you now have some self awareness about your actions. Create a goal or two dedicated to achieving more Marigold Moments and try the list again in a month. (You may create your own on a piece of paper. Fold and crease the paper vertically in three to make the columns, then open it up to write.) You will more than likely see a shift in how you feel about yourself and the relationships around you when you see the Marigold list get longer and the others get shorter!

Who do I resemble most often?

WEED	MARIGOLD!	WALNUT TREE

JOURNALING QUESTIONS

1. How have you been a Marigold for others recently?

_____

_____

_____

_____

_____

_____

_____

2. Can you think of a time when you were a Walnut Tree? Why do you think you felt the need to do this?

_____

_____

_____

_____

_____

_____

_____

3. When you think about girls in your close social circle can you identify ways in which they may have shown you different sides of themselves? When and how do they show them?

_____

_____

_____

_____

_____

_____

_____

_____

_____

_____

4. What is one goal you can set for next month to try to increase your marigold status? How will you measure that goal?

_____

_____

_____

_____

_____

_____

_____

CHAPTER 7
Is This Normal?

Relational aggression is not a new thing. Mean girls and bullies have been the topic of stories from early on. A famous Walnut Tree Girl from my childhood was Nellie Olsen from the TV series "Little House On the Prairie", based on the books by Laura Ingalls Wilder, about her life as a young pioneer girl in the 1880's traveling with her family through the Midwest. I'm ancient, so I don't expect all of you to know the series, but Laura was the daughter of a farmer, and was "friends" with a character named Nellie, the daughter of a well-to-do shop owner in town. Nellie, the perfect Walnut Tree, routinely tried to make Laura feel ashamed of her financial and social class status.

The author later revealed that Nellie was actually a combination of *several* girls with this nature she encountered in her travels. So, as you can see, relational aggression goes WAAAY back as a normal part of development from childhood to adolescence. This doesn't make it right, it just makes it true. You will see it across cultures, societies and financial sectors. It may look slightly different based on these factors, but believe me...it is still there.

WHY?

As we discussed earlier in the book, humans have a need for connection and girls especially tend to require *social* connection. The core of relational aggression is focused on isolation and exclusion of girls from certain social circles. Feeling alone and isolated during the time of adolescence is definitely a normal feeling. In fact, most teens I have worked with have felt like no one understands what they are going through at least one time in their life. Not to mention the changes that are happening in your brain during adolescence. Let me tell you, there is a LOT going on up there. As you enter your teen years, your brain starts making some decisions about what is important to keep around and what it can get rid of (called pruning).

Those few words you learned in Spanish for a visiting relative
when you were six?

GONE!

Knowing how to ride a bike?

KEEP!

Learning how to post on twitter®?

KEEP!

Logging on to Facebook®?

GONE!

(Just kidding – I'm sure your brain will never even learn that one since kids don't use Facebook anymore!)

The point is that your brain is pruning the stuff that isn't important to make way for the new stuff coming in. Here is the thing, the new stuff coming in doesn't just include facts and stuff from school. The information your "new brain" is processing also includes how to navigate your social world. There are physical changes happening where your brain is feeling more and more rewarded when you are around friends and feel accepted by them.

However, that also means that it can crash hard when you are rejected, which makes you do WHATEVER you can to avoid that isolation and rejection. This often leads to making choices you might not ordinarily make in order to stay in the group. Whether you have done it, or you have watched someone in your group do it, my guess is that you have been a part of some kind of aggression, even if you don't really know it.

Aggression is a part of the human experience. We all get angry and act aggressively at least one point in our lives. Think about the tantrums you see toddlers throwing. Usually, they involve some form of aggression (hitting, throwing things, biting, etc) because they have not learned how to mange these feelings. As we grow and develop, we begin to understand different ways of managing and dealing with these big feelings because society (and our families) frown on us just hauling off and hitting or screaming at other people when we are upset. At least after about age four; those with younger brothers and sisters know what I'm talking about!

NAMING THE BEAST

So if we can't hit, scream or throw a tantrum when we are upset, then what happens? Well, interestingly enough, there has been a lot of research around how we manage our intense feelings and the results have shown that there IS a difference between how boys and girls deal with them. Neither one gives us a good example of managing emotions effectively but understanding the difference, and how it impacts you as a person, helps us when we are ready to make different choices.

Traditionally, it has been that boys are more physical than girls in their response to conflict. They confront the person with which they are having a problem using some kind of direct statement about why they are upset. Often this may lead to increased emotions and even yelling, or possibly even a physical fight, BUT.... once it is over, they move on. Girls, on the other hand, have more of a tendency to avoid the conflict directly and use more passive aggressive techniques, like the ones we have been discussing, then hold onto the conflict for a lot longer, causing a strain in the relationship. It is thought that this happens because girls, more than boys, tend to focus more on trying to be popular and attractive than competent or talented because of that need for social acceptance. The research has shown that this shift starts to happen around age 9 or 10!!!

THAT IS CRAZY, RIGHT?

Not really, because at around this age is when a person starts to really become aware of the fact that there are ways to control and navigate their social world. However, the messages that you have been receiving about how to do this, and what it means to be a girl in the social world, have been happening since you were born. Messages are broadcasted us all the time, whether through TV, social media, billboards, parents, teachers, or just watching other adults in life. These messages shape how we think of what it means to be a boy or a girl, which causes us to internalize these messages and shapes who we are. So, as you move into the tween and teen years, you take all this information and try to make sense of it. This often leads to some stereotypes that we create about girls versus boys. Ultimately, these messages (like boys are more talented and competent in certain areas and that girls need to be pretty and popular) can often lead to lower self esteem in girls and a sense of seeking power externally, through relational aggression, instead of sourcing the power from within.

Things are beginning to change though! There has been a movement by girls and women to take some of this power back and demand equality across the board. As this shift from externally driven power to internally driven power happens, I am hopeful that future generations, like you, will begin to change the dynamic between girls and women. I am hopeful that we will support each other and lift each other up, knowing that there is room for everyone to be successful, instead of coming from the perspective that there is a limited supply of success.

So the short answer to the question, "Is this normal?", is...YES! You will find, as you meet more and more girls and women, that they have all had some kind of similar experience that you are having now. Talk to them about these experiences. Ask them questions about how they felt and how they handled it or what they might have done differently looking back. Learning from others' experiences is another way we learn how to react to our own. The thing is...

OUR EXPERIENCES SHAPE HOW WE ACT IN THIS WORLD. OUR ACTIONS SHAPE HOW WE ARE SEEN AND TREATED BY OTHERS.

Although this may be a "normal" part of girl development, my challenge to you is to dismantle the stereotypes. Take apart and dissect the messages that you have been given and challenge the way things have been done. Finding ways for girls to understand when and why relational aggression is happening in their own social circle empowers them to change the narrative which will ultimately change the social world they live in. It starts with you and your own self discovery through this book as the information you have gained begins to change the way you see yourself and others in your social circles.

Hopefully, it will help you understand that the desire for climbing the social ladder is part of the human experience, but it doesn't have to be a climb OVER each other... it can be a climb WITH each other. Hopefully, it will begin to charge your power source from within because YOU are a mighty source of power. Tap into it and you can do whatever you set your mind to!

ACTIVITIES

1. Fold half of this page back on the dotted line. Brainstorm all the messages you have received about what it means to be a girl in our society and culture. Then, keeping the page folded, turn to the back side and do the same for boys. When you are finished, open the page and look at the differences.

Ask yourself these questions:

Which messages were you given directly from your parents or other adults around you?
Which messages were never said but you understood?
Are the results what you expected?
How does it make you feel?
Do you agree with any or all of these?
How do you think these messages play a part in how you feel about yourself?

IN OUR SOCIETY, A GIRL IS...

IN OUR SOCIETY, A BOY IS...

2. Using your favorite notebook, spend one week documenting all the messages you see around you about gender and culture. Pay attention to billboards, TV ads, TV shows, movies, social media and magazines.

Each day, write down messages you see and hear about women versus men. Try to do this without judgement if you can, acting just as an observer taking data.

At the end of the week, use a highlighter to go back through your notes. Use two different-colored highlighters to do the following:

1. With one color, highlight the messages that promote a positive self image and focus on talent instead of appearance.

2. With the other color, highlight superficial messages that focus on looks or negative comments and messages about women and girls.

Ask yourself...

Did you see a difference? Did anything about the information you wrote down surprise you?

JOURNALING QUESTIONS

1. How do the girls and women in your family handle conflict with others? Is there a difference between how they handle it with the boys and men in your family versus each other?

_____

_____

_____

_____

_____

_____

2. If you have social media, take some time to look through your feed with a different set of eyes. Focus on how many posts are selfies. Are most of them boys or girls? What kinds of comments are usually posted? Were you surprised at how many posts or comments were about appearance or judgmental in some way?

_____

_____

_____

_____

_____

_____

3. How do you think these posts and comments reinforce the information you have read about in this book?

_____

_____

_____

_____

_____

_____

_____

4. What are 3 areas in your life that you have not felt confident in, in the past?

① _____

② _____

③ _____

5. What are 3 new ways you can start to use your own power to feel more self-confident in these areas?

① _____

② _____

③ _____

CHAPTER 8

Tips For Tending Your Garden

Now that you know about relational aggression, you hopefully have a better understanding of why and how girls might act the way they do. But… what now? It's one thing to read about it, but when it is happening to you it is a different story. The feelings are raw, real, and big. Often it is hard to decide how to handle certain confusing situations.

Well, I can't promise that this chapter give you ALL the answers, but what it WILL do is offer you some ideas to try and choices to make, through presenting some "tips and tricks" of handling relational aggression with other girls. Most of these ideas are built on a few core factors that lead back to everything you have learned in this book so far. These core factors are related to understanding and loving yourself, understanding the relationships around you, and finding ways to focus on your inner gamma (being authentic to who you are).

UNDERSTANDING AND LOVING YOURSELF

❀ *Find your passion!* ❀

Learning early on how to find what drives you and what you are passionate about is a gift that you give yourself. Although the things you are passionate about will change and evolve over your life, the ability to identify them is a unique way to keep inspiring you to live the best life you can. This naturally leads to your TRULY authentic self. We all have special gifts that we are born with, and discovering them is a way to honor and love who you are as well as those around you. When this happens and you tap into your unique gifts, a love of self follows naturally. BONUS…people around you benefit from your awesome talents!

We all have passions, but somewhere along the way we start to lose focus of them. When we are young children, we always know what they are, but as we get older, other influences (like what people think of us) start to make us avoid things we may love to do. Embracing your passion and unique gifts is a direct line to self-love and acceptance! Use these questions to find your way back to some passions you have inside you.

♡ What are the things you love to do?

♡ What are the things you love about yourself?

♡ Besides social media, what is something you do or think about that makes you lose all track of time?

♡ When you have free time, what is the thing that you usually find yourself doing or wanting to do?

♡ If you had all the money and time in the world and no one would know what you were doing, what would you do?

❀ *Learn how to accept compliments!* ❀

We talked about this in chapter 3, but it is worth revisiting because of the importance of this topic. As girls and women, we often have difficulty accepting compliments from others. Here is what I want you to think about:

WHEN YOU REFUSE A COMPLIMENT FROM ANOTHER PERSON, YOU ARE NOT ONLY GIVING THEM THE MESSAGE THAT YOU THINK THEIR OPINION IS WRONG, YOU ARE ALSO GIVING YOURSELF THE MESSAGE THAT YOU ARE NOT WORTHY OF THAT POSITIVE THING THEY SAID ABOUT YOU.

Not only that, but there is actually some mind/body science behind the negative self talk we do when responding to a compliment that way. Chronic negative self-talk has been shown to increased stress hormones and even lead to feelings of sadness and depression which can ultimately lead to low self esteem. It is also worth mentioning that when you look and speak to the world in a negative way, it starts to impact the way you see yourself in the world AND how the world sees you.

When negative statements start to become larger parts of your conversations, then it leads to decreased motivation to do things and even have less interaction with friends (either because you choose not to because you feel bad about yourself or because they don't like being around negative statements all the time). On the flip side, when you learn to accept compliments (even if you don't believe them at first) it triggers something in your brain to stop that negative thinking. As you shift to positive self-talk, you are happier and the people around you notice.

Now…let me say this; I KNOW how hard this is! Accepting compliments is one of the hardest things to do at times. So, when your initial reaction starts with, "Thanks, BUT…", challenge yourself to STOP, REWIND and just say, "THANK YOU!" It sounds easy but it takes a lot of practice. I still have to catch myself all the time with this one. Using those two simple words without adding *anything* is hard, however I can tell you that once you start to do it you will begin to see a difference in how you feel about yourself and you may even influence others to do the same just by doing it yourself.

Just say… THANK YOU!

❀ *Learn how to forgive yourself!* ❀

This is a biggie! As girls, we are often taught that we should forgive others. "Say you're sorry" is a big part of the language we are taught growing up. But think back for a minute at conversations you have had with people around you (teachers, parents, other adults). Has anyone every said to you, "Forgive yourself"? My bet is that, for most of us, this is not something we hear often.

It is actually a bit of a weird concept, forgiving yourself. How do I say sorry to myself? You do it JUST LIKE THAT! You literally have a conversation with yourself either verbally (I suggest you do it when no one is around or you might get a few weird looks) or through writing. But the catch is, you have to make it happen outside of your own thoughts. By putting it down on paper or saying it out loud, it becomes more of a reality, and you kind of trick your brain into believing it. When we just think about things we want to say, they can easily be tossed out of our mind.

Say it or write it

I have actually taken time, in the past, to sit and write a letter to myself explaining what I did and why I forgive myself, as well as the lesson I learned. You can take the same concept that you were taught about how to apologize to others and use it on yourself. Try this yourself by imagining that the issue happened with your best friend then writing a letter to her about it. What would you tell her? After you finish go back and replace her name with yours!

You might be asking, "Why on earth would I do this?" Good question! Here is the thing… part of understanding and loving yourself involves embracing all of the faults we have as well. There is a quote that goes something like this…

A man is whole only when he takes into account his shadow.

- Djuna Barnes

What this means is that by embracing the mistakes we make (the shadow or dark side of who we are) and acknowledging the negative parts of who we are, we develop into a stronger "whole" person that is ultimately able to love ourselves and live a happier, more fulfilled life. Part of this is being able to not only recognize when we have done something to hurt ourselves, but to forgive ourselves for doing it.

Now, this is much easier said than done, especially if it is something that you don't normally do now. Taking the steps to forgive yourself for something can be awkward and uncomfortable, but I promise that if you practice this you will find it helps you uncover some truly amazing things about yourself as you grow into the amazing human you are meant to be!

You're ACES!

We tend to treat others with more compassion than we treat ourselves. Have you ever heard the phrase, "She is her own worst critic?" It means that you are harder on yourself than anyone else, or, no one criticizes you more than you do yourself. In order to practice self forgiveness, we have to have a compassionate conversation with our own inner critic to tell her it is ok to chill out just a little!

When something happens and you find yourself obsessing over what you did wrong or feeling bad about something you said or did, you can use the steps on the following page.

You're Aces!

Achieving Balance

We all play a role in our relationships. When a conflict arises it is important to take a minute to recognize what role we played in it, but to also understand that it is never 100% our fault. Taking responsibility for your part, but not all of it, is balanced. By stopping to think about what roles everyone played, we are able to look at it from a larger, more accurate viewpoint.

Change the Way You Talk to Yourself

When something happens and we blame ourselves, we usually tend to say negative things about ourselves. I have heard things like, "I'm so stupid" or "I suck at that" or "I'm an idiot". This is called negative self-talk and it doesn't do anything to help you. In fact, it does the opposite; it only reinforces those thoughts of how bad you are. Instead, turn those statements on their head and state the opposite. For example, instead of "I suck at that" try, "I am still learning" followed by what you might try differently next time. Understand that mistakes don't define you, rather they build who you are. Learn from your mistakes and you build a strong foundation for those skills.

Embrace a Different Story

Think about what happened and what you can do differently next time. You can't change the past but you CAN learn from it and use some of these things you learned in the future. Creating a different story helps you to form ideas of how to handle the situation in the future. It doesn't change what has already happened but it helps you formulate a plan of action for later.

Show Kindness and Compassion for Yourself

If this happened with your best friend and they did what you did, then came to ask your forgiveness…what would you say to them? Take a moment and write a sentence or two:

_____

_____

_____

My guess is that your response involved some form of kindness and compassion, right? Take a moment and read it to yourself. This is your own message of kindness and compassion that you need to hear from yourself.

CLIP THIS PAGE OUT AND PUT IT
SOMEWHERE YOU'LL SEE OFTEN!

❀ *Build your self-confidence!* ❀

What does it mean to be self-confident? There are many definitions but basically, being self-confident means feeling good about your abilities, appearance and self in general. Take a minute to use the checklist below to see where you fall in your own self-confidence.

CHECKLIST OF SELF-CONFIDENT BEHAVIORS

Confident

- ☐ STANDS STRAIGHT
- ☐ GOOD EYE CONTACT WHEN SPEAKING
- ☐ MAINTAINS BALANCED RELATIONSHIPS
- ☐ SPEAKS UP WHEN THEY WANT TO
- ☐ IS ABLE TO SHARE IDEAS WITHOUT WORRY
- ☐ DOESN'T SHY AWAY FROM DEBATES
- ☐ USES A CLEAR, CALM TONE OF VOICE
- ☐ ADVOCATES FOR WHAT THEY THINK EVEN IF IT'S DIFFERENT FROM THE GROUP
- ☐ HANDLES CRITICISM BY BEING INQUISITIVE AND EAGER TO LEARN FROM IT
- ☐ TAKES CARE OF THEMSELVES AND FEELS COMFORTABLE STANDING OUT

Not Confident

- ☐ SLUMPED SHOULDERS
- ☐ LOOKS DOWN OR AWAY WHEN TALKING
- ☐ OFTEN APOLOGIZES FOR THINGS
- ☐ DOESN'T USUALLY START CONVERSATIONS
- ☐ LETS PEOPLE INTERRUPT OFTEN
- ☐ CAVES IN EASILY IN A DISAGREEMENT
- ☐ USES A SOFT VOICE (WHINE OR WOBBLY)
- ☐ GOES ALONG WITH THE GROUP INSTEAD OF STATING THOUGHTS AND BELIEFS
- ☐ CAN BECOME VERY DEFENSIVE WHEN SOMEONE CRITIQUES OR CRITICIZES THEM
- ☐ TRIES TO "BLEND IN" AS MUCH AS POSSIBLE

How did you do? Did you have more checkmarks in the confident or not confident area? Neither one is wrong, it just helps you understand where your current level of self confidence might be, which will help you figure out how to add more checkmarks to the confident box in the future. The first step in increasing your self confidence is to find ways to show yourself self-love and be able to laugh at yourself. Self-confidence is not something someone else can give or take away from you – it is generated ONLY by you and you have control over how much you keep and give away.

UNDERSTANDING THE RELATIONSHIPS AROUND YOU

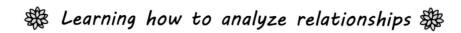

❁ *Learning how to analyze relationships* ❁

We have done a lot of work in this area in previous chapters but this is repeated here because it is such an important part of this process. By understanding the people around you and what role they play in your life, you are able to see things more objectively; like taking off an emotional blindfold. This allows you to put the puzzle together in different ways in order to challenge the thoughts and beliefs you had about certain situations when feelings were running the show.

So, when you are feeling overwhelmed with relationships around you, take a moment to use the tools on the following two pages and review them with your other tools and reflective questions.

My Marigolds

A garden is only as strong as its roots and each marigold has a system of support surrounding them. Take some time every so often to complete this activity in order to evaluate who your strongest supports are around you.

Brainstorm all the people in your life that support you and place their names on the roots of your marigolds in your garden. If they are a stronger support make sure to place them on the larger flowers with thick roots that are deep and established. Consider clipping this page out of the book and placing the graphic in your room or personal space that is visible so you can see it every day to remind you of the people that you can go to when you need it.

Getting To Know What My Garden Grows

This is designed to help you lay out the roles of the girls in your group. Write down the girls' names and roles in the spaces provided. In this graphic, you may or not may not have a victim or "seed" character, as there are some groups of friends that don't necessarily have a victim in their group, but instead, each of the girls rotate as the victim of a Walnut Tree's aggression. In this case, you can list more than one girl or you can choose to just leave that portion out.

Reflective Questions!

What are you looking for in a good friend? Does this person give you that?

What is it about this particular friend that makes you feel like this?

When a friend does something that is hurtful, ask yourself what message she might be sending you. If you allow her to act this way to you, what message are *you* sending *her* about *you*?

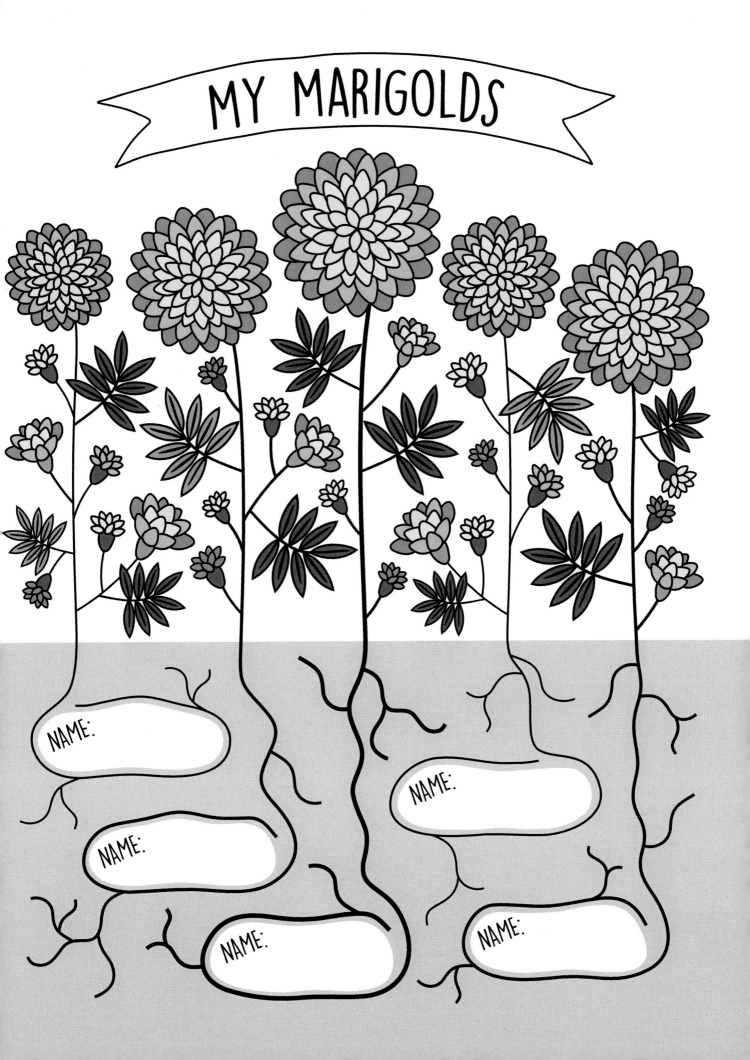

CLIP THIS PAGE OUT AND PUT IT
SOMEWHERE YOU'LL SEE OFTEN!

Marigolds

Always true to themselves, these protective, nurturing, honest friends spread positive energy wherever they go. I want to grow many of them and plant myself nearby!

_____

_____

Daffodils & Snowdrops

Friends, family and others around us that may not share all of our same interests, but can still be supportive, positive influences that attract good things to the garden – like, Marigolds!

_____

_____

Daisies

Nice girls that tend to wilt under Walnut Trees and not remain true to themselves.

_____

_____

WEEDS

Annoying girls in the middle of everything, pot-stirrers that seek approval from Walnut Trees.

_____

_____

Seeds

Victims of poisonous Walnut Trees and their frightened followers – Daisies and Weeds.

_____

_____

Walnut Trees

Leaders of gardens who are mean, bossy girls. They are insecure and control others to feel powerful.

_____

_____

CLIP THIS PAGE OUT AND PUT IT
SOMEWHERE YOU'LL SEE OFTEN!

FINDING WAYS TO BRING THE FOCUS BACK TO YOUR INNER GAMMA
(BEING AUTHENTIC TO WHO YOU ARE)

❀ *Responding to relational aggressive behavior* ❀

When responding to a Walnut Tree, our first response is usually to react out of emotion. This reaction is usually based on raw emotion, with little to no logical thinking. (That is normal for most people, by the way.)

After we react, we then tend to isolate in some form and think about what happened. This is usually when that logical part of our brain takes over and asks, "What just happened here? What did you do and what will happen next?" And just like that, we turn into Alice in Wonderland and fall down the rabbit hole of anxiety, thinking about all the horrible things that will happen because of the way we reacted to this situation.

Now…imagine the same situation but this time you don't react first. Instead, you leave (even isolate) first and use the tools we talked about previously to think about the situation that happened. You try to make sense of the situation based on your knowledge of the Marigold Girl and Walnut Tree Girl theory, and then create a plan to respond based on what you came up with.

This doesn't mean you can't go home and FREAK OUT for a bit, letting those emotions fly. But you do it in a safe place and once you have let those go , your logical thinking brain moves into the driver's seat.

① Leave

② LET OUT EMOTION!

③ LET IN LOGICAL THINKING!

④ Respond

Similarly, sometimes it may not be aggressive behavior that is clearly the problem, but you may feel some serious *peer pressure* to do something that makes you uncomfortable. In these cases, try any of these responses to help you stay true to YOU.

STICK TO YOUR GUNS WITH RESPECTFUL HONESTY

Pick your stance and stick with it. You can say the same thing in different ways if needed.

 No thanks, I don't want to do it.   *I can't be a part of making her feel bad.*

ASK QUESTIONS

Questions are unexpected with people applying peer pressure. It often will throw them off their game because they were not prepared to answer questions that challenge them. Be prepared though that sometimes their response might be to get angry or mean because they either get embarrassed that they don't have an answer or you are not doing what they want you to do. In these cases, just be as kind as you can in your response and move back to number one (stick to your guns and leave if needed).

 Why do you want to do that?   *Why are you asking me?*
What is the purpose of it?   *How does that help?*

KEEP THE FRIENDSHIP OPEN

Let them know that you don't agree with their choices but that you still want to be friends when they decide to make different choices.

 I don't want to do that, but if you change your mind, let me know!

THIS is what it means to bring your focus back to your inner gamma. It won't happen every time, but even if you are able to practice this skill a *few* times it might start to become easier and happen more and more.

The difference between passive, aggressive and assertive

The way we respond to others in getting our needs met both emotionally and physically is a VERY important tool to master. It takes practice and if you are not a naturally assertive person you might find that strengthening this social muscle will be something you have to work on for awhile, but once you master it you are GOLDEN.

Understanding how to use assertiveness is a bit of a superpower once you understand it. It not only empowers you each time you use it effectively, but as you move into adulthood, this is a tool that will open doors and create strong, foundational relationships with friends and coworkers.

So, what's the difference between these types of behavior?

Passive

This is where you basically do NOTHING. You try to blend into your surroundings and hope you don't get called out by someone to participate. With passivity, other people often decide what is going to happen and you do not use a voice to advocate for what you want or need. This can cause feelings of helplessness, a lack of control over your own life, and make you feel small or insignificant. Definitely *not* a place of confidence. Often, you will see passivity in someone when you see some of these behaviors:

Difficulty making eye contact   Agrees with most everyone
Slumped shoulders   Apologizes a lot   Uses "I don't know"

Aggressive

Getting your needs met whatever way necessary, without consideration for the thoughts or feelings of others. When you are aggressive you can be pushy and don't listen to others, with a "win at all costs" mentality that doesn't take into account the needs of others. A general lack of respect is both given and received. Their behaviors can cause them loneliness, anger and hostility, and feelings of isolation after they get what they want. Some of the behaviors you see may include:

Uses body posturing and voice tone to gain power
Interrupts often   Clenches fists or jaw
Uses sarcasm and put downs
Appears insensitive   Raises voice or yelling
Often invades personal space or boundaries
Argues a lot and is easily triggered by a different opinion

Assertive

Getting your needs met without hurting another person by stating your thoughts and feelings in an appropriate yet clear way. You stand up for what you want, need, or believe but still show respect for yourself and others. You are clear, honest and direct in the message you are giving to the other person and then make them feel heard as well. When you are assertive in your communication with others you usually feel confident and proud. You develop a respect *for* yourself and *from* others and begin to develop a reputation of honesty and trust among peers. Assertive behavior often looks like:

Makes eye contact   Uses a calm voice tone   Uses active listening skills
Speaks needs clearly   Stands tall

Assertive Behavior Breakdown

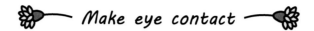 Make eye contact

Making eye contact doesn't mean you have to KEEP eye contact – staring is not the best option here. However, looking someone in the eye when they speak to you or when you speak to them (in a way you would when speaking with others in any other conversation) is appropriate. The point here is really to just make sure you are not looking down or away. Appropriate eye contact helps the person you are talking to understand that you are listening to them.

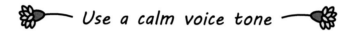 Use a calm voice tone

This does NOT mean meek and soft, it means stating your thoughts in a clear even tone without yelling, raising your voice or talking fast.

 Use active listening skills

You are letting the person know that they are heard. You also show interest in what the other person is saying by looking at the person who is speaking and nodding your head when you understand what the person is saying. You can also show you are interested by asking questions. You should ask questions so that you are sure you understand what was said.

 Verbalize needs clearly

Get clear on what you want or need from the conversation. This may mean that you have to plan it out ahead of time. You don't need a script to follow but you do need to be able to know what it is that you want as a solution as well as what compromises you might be willing to make. It is OK to ask for what you need and when you get it that does not mean that the other person is losing out. In fact, it is the opposite, by verbalizing what you need, it often helps the other person come to realize that they might need something as well which leads to a more authentic (there is that word again) discussion. Honest talk leads to heartfelt solutions!

Stand tall

You don't have to stand in a wonder woman pose while you are talking but if you slouch or try to get small you often lose the ability to do the other things on this list. Body posture is another way to trick your brain into feeling confident. So just try to be aware of keeping your shoulders back and head up while you are speaking.

One way to remind yourself of how to use these skills, is to do **LAST**:

Listen with active listening skills to understand what the other person needs
Acknowledge what you heard to validate that you understand their needs
Share your thought or idea in a clear and honest way
Together, find a solution that meets both your needs

Now, realistically, the "T" portion of this model might not always happen. It may be that in certain cases you have to walk away without a solution that meets both your needs. In these cases, you need to give yourself permission to be ok with that. There will be times that you will have to "agree to disagree" with other people. This is a solution in itself in some situations and as long as you can part ways respectfully and no one is hurt, this might be the only solution. This doesn't mean that it can *never* be resolved, but for now…it is okay!

By using these skills in situations that don't involve your friend groups, you will find opportunities to build these skills without worrying about how it might impact your social life. Practice using assertiveness in a lot of different situations that don't involve your friends. Here are just a few of the places you might be able to practice your assertiveness skills outside of your friendships:

Asking for help in a bookstore
Placing an order in a restaurant
Checking out when shopping
Sending food back in a restaurant
Advocating for something you want from your parents

🌸 *Mastering the art of negotiation* 🌸

Negotiating happens every day in many situations, but oftentimes, we don't even know it is happening. If life happened without negotiation we would live in a world of constant fighting, as people would only be focused on their own needs. However, we learn from an early age that, in most circumstances, negotiating our way to our goal is the fastest way to get there. However, most of us are never really educated on how to do that! In order to be authentic to who you are and find ways to manage the Walnut Trees around you, negotiation is a key skill to master for use in a variety of situations. Here is an example of the steps it takes to make it work:

🌸 Face the other person, giving eye contact.

🌸 Monitor your voice tone (not too loud or soft), facial expression and body posture (straight or relaxed).

🌸 Use active listening skills to hear what the other person is asking for.

🌸 Use a clear and honest statement to ask for what you want and why you want it.

🌸 Evaluate whether you are in agreement or not.

>   IF YOU AGREE
>   Thank the other person if he or she agrees to the request.
>
>   IF YOU DO NOT AGREE
>   Suggest a compromise and thank them if they agree.
>   Ask the other person for a solution if he or she does not agree with the compromise and thank them if you agree.

🌸 If you still cannot agree, ask them to take some time to think about other solutions and plan a time to come back together to discuss again.

❀ Developing Grit and Resilience ❀

What are grit and resilience and why are they important? Well, these two things often go together. Grit is defined as having perseverance for goals you have set. Resilience is defined as the ability to address and overcome challenges, adversity and stress.

In other words, facing your problems, evaluating your choices, choosing a solution to try, and then NOT GIVING UP until you find the right solution.

This is an easier concept to apply in real life with things that don't have emotion involved. Things like schoolwork or learning a skill (instrument, bike riding, etc). However, once you add emotions into the mix....it takes it to another level.

Many times, girls that fall into the Walnut Tree category have not developed good resilience. Think about this...when girls don't have a strong sense of resilience they fall back on being mean to others because they don't know how to deal with their own feelings of failure; it is easier to take out those negative feelings on others. This is important to know because it not only helps you to see why *you* should develop your own resilience, but it can help you understand why *another person* may be acting the way *they* are as well.

I will be the first to admit that this concept of grit and resilience in working with other people, especially when you are in the throws of adolescence, is a BIG challenge. It is probably one of the more difficult areas in this chapter that I am proposing. That being said, it is a tool that will not only help you navigate and problem solve NOW with friend drama, but it is a skill that can, and will, be really appreciated as you move into adulthood. A lot of people that have fine-tuned their grit and resilience have used it to develop companies, new inventions, or even found discoveries in our universe. It is a tool that takes a long time to master, but being able to keep going despite life's roadblocks and speed bumps that pop up is a secret tool that will help you build success in many areas. Here is how it works...

When something pops up as a problem, think about using a **FILTER**:
FIND the problem
INVESTIGATE all the choices you have to respond to it
LIST the pros and cons for the choices you identified
TRY /Choose the one you want to try
EVALUATE what might happen with the choice you made
(think of all options good and bad), then try it out.
REVIEW whether or not it worked the way you expected and if you want to use it again

Use this model whenever you run into a problem to help you gain some objective view of what is happening. It may be that you have to use it a few times with the same problem. Don't stress, that is normal! Many times we have to try out different solutions to the same problem. You might even find that the problem changes just a little based on the first or second solution you tried. Don't give up! This is where the magic happens. As you do this, you will see a shift happen not only in the problem itself, but in the way you feel about how you go about solving problems that come your way. You will start to see them as a challenge or riddle to be solved and move away from taking things personally because it no longer becomes about "what did I do wrong". Instead, it moves to "what can I try to solve this issue". This helps us take the focus off ourselves and moves it to a more neutral thing, like the problem itself.

So let's take a hot minute to recap this last big chapter in a nutshell! When you are navigating the big issues with friends, you will have a much easier time of it when you have mastered these...

THREE BIG SKILLS!

① UNDERSTANDING AND LOVING YOURSELF!

② UNDERSTANDING THE RELATIONSHIPS AROUND YOU!

③ FOCUSING ON YOUR INNER GAMMA — BEING AUTHENTIC TO WHO YOU ARE!

You can do this with PRACTICE, PRACTICE, PRACTICE in the following areas!

Finding what you are passionate about.

Accepting compliments.

Using the ACES acronym to bring in the logical brain.

Reviewing the people around you every so often to see who your Marigolds are and those who might not be so healthy.

Using assertiveness and negotiation skills.

Problem solving using grit and resilience.

YOU MADE IT TO THE END!

I know you just sorted through a *lot* of information. My hope is that you will come back to this book whenever you have challenges, and use the tools to help move toward a clear mind and peaceful heart in this time of crazy growth. You are stepping into an amazing time in your life. Using these tools will not only help you navigate the friendships around you today, but through practice, you will find that you can use them throughout life, well after you graduate and move on to a life of your own.

I use many of these every day, and truth be told... I *still* have to remind and challenge myself to use them. I practice exactly what I have shared here with my daughters, friends, coworkers and family today. I don't always do it perfectly and don't always do it consistently...but I do it! And when I succeed, my confidence grows, I am happier and I surround myself with people that support me for being ME.

That is my wish for you!

Dr. Kim

If you want to continue this journey, please visit our website to stay up-to-date on new information. This is an ongoing project to encourage collaboration, sharing and learning between girls and women that want to build a garden of support. We would love to hear from you and have you plant your foot in our garden.

WWW.MARIGOLDGIRLS.COM

Now, go do YOU...because YOU are MAGICAL!

30 DAY JOURNAL

The
Marigold Challenge!

Now that you have read the book and worked
your way through the activities, I encourage
you to take the 30 Day Marigold Challenge.
Take a few minutes each day to reflect on
and practice your Marigold skills.

❋ Date:

_____

❋ What new goal or intention did you set out to try today?

_____

❋ Did you achieve it? If not, how will you change it to try again tomorrow?

_____

_____

❋ What were some challenges that came up today?

_____

_____

❋ How can you use a different lens (objectively) to see this situation differently?

_____

❋ What were some tips/tricks that you tried today? What worked and didn't work?

_____

_____

❋ Can you think of why they may have not worked? What would you change?

_____

_____

❋ Who was there for you today when you needed them?

_____

❋ How did you practice being assertive today? How did it feel?

_____

_____

❋ What was a proud moment for you today?

_____

_____

❋ What are you grateful for today?

_____

✿ Date:
_____

✿ What new goal or intention did you set out to try today?

_____

✿ Did you achieve it? If not, how will you change it to try again tomorrow?

_____

_____

✿ What were some challenges that came up today?

_____

_____

✿ How can you use a different lens (objectively) to see this situation differently?

_____

✿ What were some tips/tricks that you tried today? What worked and didn't work?

_____

_____

✿ Can you think of why they may have not worked? What would you change?

_____

_____

✿ Who was there for you today when you needed them?

_____

✿ How did you practice being assertive today? How did it feel?

_____

_____

✿ What was a proud moment for you today?

_____

_____

✿ What are you grateful for today?

_____

Day 2

❀ Date:
_____

❀ What new goal or intention did you set out to try today?

_____

❀ Did you achieve it? If not, how will you change it to try again tomorrow?

_____

_____

❀ What were some challenges that came up today?

_____

_____

❀ How can you use a different lens (objectively) to see this situation differently?

_____

❀ What were some tips/tricks that you tried today? What worked and didn't work?

_____

_____

❀ Can you think of why they may have not worked? What would you change?

_____

_____

❀ Who was there for you today when you needed them?

_____

❀ How did you practice being assertive today? How did it feel?

_____

_____

❀ What was a proud moment for you today?

_____

_____

❀ What are you grateful for today?

_____

✿ Date:

_____

✿ What new goal or intention did you set out to try today?

_____

✿ Did you achieve it? If not, how will you change it to try again tomorrow?

_____

_____

✿ What were some challenges that came up today?

_____

_____

✿ How can you use a different lens (objectively) to see this situation differently?

_____

✿ What were some tips/tricks that you tried today? What worked and didn't work?

_____

_____

✿ Can you think of why they may have not worked? What would you change?

_____

_____

✿ Who was there for you today when you needed them?

_____

✿ How did you practice being assertive today? How did it feel?

_____

_____

✿ What was a proud moment for you today?

_____

_____

✿ What are you grateful for today?

_____

❀ Date:
_____

❀ What new goal or intention did you set out to try today?
_____

❀ Did you achieve it? If not, how will you change it to try again tomorrow?
_____
_____

❀ What were some challenges that came up today?
_____
_____

❀ How can you use a different lens (objectively) to see this situation differently?
_____

❀ What were some tips/tricks that you tried today? What worked and didn't work?
_____
_____

❀ Can you think of why they may have not worked? What would you change?
_____
_____
_____

❀ Who was there for you today when you needed them?
_____

❀ How did you practice being assertive today? How did it feel?
_____
_____

❀ What was a proud moment for you today?
_____
_____

❀ What are you grateful for today?
_____

❀ Date:
_____

❀ What new goal or intention did you set out to try today?

_____

❀ Did you achieve it? If not, how will you change it to try again tomorrow?

_____

_____

❀ What were some challenges that came up today?

_____

_____

❀ How can you use a different lens (objectively) to see this situation differently?

_____

❀ What were some tips/tricks that you tried today? What worked and didn't work?

_____

_____

❀ Can you think of why they may have not worked? What would you change?

_____

_____

❀ Who was there for you today when you needed them?

_____

❀ How did you practice being assertive today? How did it feel?

_____

_____

❀ What was a proud moment for you today?

_____

_____

❀ What are you grateful for today?

_____

❀ Date:
_____

❀ **Day 7**

❀ What new goal or intention did you set out to try today?

_____

❀ Did you achieve it? If not, how will you change it to try again tomorrow?

_____

_____

❀ What were some challenges that came up today?

_____

_____

❀ How can you use a different lens (objectively) to see this situation differently?

_____

❀ What were some tips/tricks that you tried today? What worked and didn't work?

_____

_____

❀ Can you think of why they may have not worked? What would you change?

_____

_____

❀ Who was there for you today when you needed them?

_____

❀ How did you practice being assertive today? How did it feel?

_____

_____

❀ What was a proud moment for you today?

_____

_____

❀ What are you grateful for today?

_____

Date:

_____

❀ What new goal or intention did you set out to try today?

_____

❀ Did you achieve it? If not, how will you change it to try again tomorrow?

_____

_____

❀ What were some challenges that came up today?

_____

_____

❀ How can you use a different lens (objectively) to see this situation differently?

_____

❀ What were some tips/tricks that you tried today? What worked and didn't work?

_____

_____

❀ Can you think of why they may have not worked? What would you change?

_____

_____

❀ Who was there for you today when you needed them?

_____

❀ How did you practice being assertive today? How did it feel?

_____

_____

❀ What was a proud moment for you today?

_____

_____

❀ What are you grateful for today?

_____

❀ Date:

_____

❀ What new goal or intention did you set out to try today?

_____

❀ Did you achieve it? If not, how will you change it to try again tomorrow?

_____

_____

❀ What were some challenges that came up today?

_____

_____

❀ How can you use a different lens (objectively) to see this situation differently?

_____

❀ What were some tips/tricks that you tried today? What worked and didn't work?

_____

_____

❀ Can you think of why they may have not worked? What would you change?

_____

_____

❀ Who was there for you today when you needed them?

_____

❀ How did you practice being assertive today? How did it feel?

_____

_____

❀ What was a proud moment for you today?

_____

_____

❀ What are you grateful for today?

_____

❀ Date:

_____

❀ What new goal or intention did you set out to try today?

_____

❀ Did you achieve it? If not, how will you change it to try again tomorrow?

_____

_____

❀ What were some challenges that came up today?

_____

_____

❀ How can you use a different lens (objectively) to see this situation differently?

_____

❀ What were some tips/tricks that you tried today? What worked and didn't work?

_____

_____

❀ Can you think of why they may have not worked? What would you change?

_____

_____

❀ Who was there for you today when you needed them?

_____

❀ How did you practice being assertive today? How did it feel?

_____

_____

❀ What was a proud moment for you today?

_____

_____

❀ What are you grateful for today?

_____

❀ Date:
_____

Day 11

❀ What new goal or intention did you set out to try today?
_____

❀ Did you achieve it? If not, how will you change it to try again tomorrow?
_____
_____

❀ What were some challenges that came up today?
_____
_____

❀ How can you use a different lens (objectively) to see this situation differently?
_____

❀ What were some tips/tricks that you tried today? What worked and didn't work?
_____
_____

❀ Can you think of why they may have not worked? What would you change?
_____
_____

❀ Who was there for you today when you needed them?
_____

❀ How did you practice being assertive today? How did it feel?
_____
_____

❀ What was a proud moment for you today?
_____
_____

❀ What are you grateful for today?
_____

Date:

_____

What new goal or intention did you set out to try today?

_____

Did you achieve it? If not, how will you change it to try again tomorrow?

_____

_____

What were some challenges that came up today?

_____

_____

How can you use a different lens (objectively) to see this situation differently?

_____

What were some tips/tricks that you tried today? What worked and didn't work?

_____

_____

Can you think of why they may have not worked? What would you change?

_____

_____

Who was there for you today when you needed them?

_____

How did you practice being assertive today? How did it feel?

_____

_____

What was a proud moment for you today?

_____

_____

What are you grateful for today?

_____

Day 12

❀ Date:

_____

❀ What new goal or intention did you set out to try today?

_____

❀ Did you achieve it? If not, how will you change it to try again tomorrow?

_____

_____

❀ What were some challenges that came up today?

_____

_____

❀ How can you use a different lens (objectively) to see this situation differently?

_____

❀ What were some tips/tricks that you tried today? What worked and didn't work?

_____

_____

❀ Can you think of why they may have not worked? What would you change?

_____

_____

❀ Who was there for you today when you needed them?

_____

❀ How did you practice being assertive today? How did it feel?

_____

_____

❀ What was a proud moment for you today?

_____

_____

❀ What are you grateful for today?

_____

❀ Date:

_____

❀ What new goal or intention did you set out to try today?

_____

❀ Did you achieve it? If not, how will you change it to try again tomorrow?

_____

_____

❀ What were some challenges that came up today?

_____

_____

❀ How can you use a different lens (objectively) to see this situation differently?

_____

❀ What were some tips/tricks that you tried today? What worked and didn't work?

_____

_____

❀ Can you think of why they may have not worked? What would you change?

_____

_____

❀ Who was there for you today when you needed them?

_____

❀ How did you practice being assertive today? How did it feel?

_____

_____

❀ What was a proud moment for you today?

_____

_____

❀ What are you grateful for today?

_____

❀ *Day 14*

❋ Date:
_____

❋ What new goal or intention did you set out to try today?

_____

❋ Did you achieve it? If not, how will you change it to try again tomorrow?

_____

_____

❋ What were some challenges that came up today?

_____

_____

❋ How can you use a different lens (objectively) to see this situation differently?

_____

❋ What were some tips/tricks that you tried today? What worked and didn't work?

_____

_____

❋ Can you think of why they may have not worked? What would you change?

_____

_____

❋ Who was there for you today when you needed them?

_____

❋ How did you practice being assertive today? How did it feel?

_____

_____

❋ What was a proud moment for you today?

_____

_____

❋ What are you grateful for today?

_____

❊ Date:

_____

❊ What new goal or intention did you set out to try today?

_____

❊ Did you achieve it? If not, how will you change it to try again tomorrow?

_____

_____

❊ What were some challenges that came up today?

_____

_____

❊ How can you use a different lens (objectively) to see this situation differently?

_____

❊ What were some tips/tricks that you tried today? What worked and didn't work?

_____

_____

❊ Can you think of why they may have not worked? What would you change?

_____

_____

❊ Who was there for you today when you needed them?

_____

❊ How did you practice being assertive today? How did it feel?

_____

_____

❊ What was a proud moment for you today?

_____

_____

❊ What are you grateful for today?

_____

❀ Date:

_____

❀ What new goal or intention did you set out to try today?

_____

❀ Day 17

❀ Did you achieve it? If not, how will you change it to try again tomorrow?

_____

_____

❀ What were some challenges that came up today?

_____

_____

❀ How can you use a different lens (objectively) to see this situation differently?

_____

❀ What were some tips/tricks that you tried today? What worked and didn't work?

_____

_____

❀ Can you think of why they may have not worked? What would you change?

_____

_____

❀ Who was there for you today when you needed them?

_____

❀ How did you practice being assertive today? How did it feel?

_____

_____

❀ What was a proud moment for you today?

_____

_____

❀ What are you grateful for today?

_____

❊ Date:

_____

❊ What new goal or intention did you set out to try today?

_____

❊ Did you achieve it? If not, how will you change it to try again tomorrow?

_____

_____

❊ What were some challenges that came up today?

_____

_____

❊ How can you use a different lens (objectively) to see this situation differently?

_____

❊ What were some tips/tricks that you tried today? What worked and didn't work?

_____

_____

❊ Can you think of why they may have not worked? What would you change?

_____

_____

❊ Who was there for you today when you needed them?

_____

❊ How did you practice being assertive today? How did it feel?

_____

_____

❊ What was a proud moment for you today?

_____

_____

❊ What are you grateful for today?

_____

Day 18

❀ Date:
_____

❀ What new goal or intention did you set out to try today?

_____

❀ Did you achieve it? If not, how will you change it to try again tomorrow?

_____

_____

❀ What were some challenges that came up today?

_____

_____

❀ How can you use a different lens (objectively) to see this situation differently?

_____

❀ What were some tips/tricks that you tried today? What worked and didn't work?

_____

_____

❀ Can you think of why they may have not worked? What would you change?

_____

_____

_____

❀ Who was there for you today when you needed them?

_____

❀ How did you practice being assertive today? How did it feel?

_____

_____

_____

❀ What was a proud moment for you today?

_____

_____

❀ What are you grateful for today?

_____

Date:

_____

❋ What new goal or intention did you set out to try today?

_____

❋ Did you achieve it? If not, how will you change it to try again tomorrow?

_____

_____

❋ What were some challenges that came up today?

_____

_____

❋ How can you use a different lens (objectively) to see this situation differently?

_____

❋ What were some tips/tricks that you tried today? What worked and didn't work?

_____

_____

❋ Can you think of why they may have not worked? What would you change?

_____

_____

❋ Who was there for you today when you needed them?

_____

❋ How did you practice being assertive today? How did it feel?

_____

_____

❋ What was a proud moment for you today?

_____

_____

❋ What are you grateful for today?

_____

❀ Date:

_____

❀ Day 21

❀ What new goal or intention did you set out to try today?

_____

❀ Did you achieve it? If not, how will you change it to try again tomorrow?

_____

_____

❀ What were some challenges that came up today?

_____

_____

❀ How can you use a different lens (objectively) to see this situation differently?

_____

❀ What were some tips/tricks that you tried today? What worked and didn't work?

_____

_____

❀ Can you think of why they may have not worked? What would you change?

_____

_____

❀ Who was there for you today when you needed them?

_____

❀ How did you practice being assertive today? How did it feel?

_____

_____

❀ What was a proud moment for you today?

_____

_____

❀ What are you grateful for today?

_____

❀ Date:
_____

❀ What new goal or intention did you set out to try today?

_____

❀ Did you achieve it? If not, how will you change it to try again tomorrow?

_____

_____

❀ What were some challenges that came up today?

_____

_____

❀ How can you use a different lens (objectively) to see this situation differently?

_____

❀ What were some tips/tricks that you tried today? What worked and didn't work?

_____

_____

❀ Can you think of why they may have not worked? What would you change?

_____

_____

❀ Who was there for you today when you needed them?

_____

❀ How did you practice being assertive today? How did it feel?

_____

_____

❀ What was a proud moment for you today?

_____

_____

❀ What are you grateful for today?

_____

❀ Date:
_____

❀ What new goal or intention did you set out to try today?

_____

❀ Did you achieve it? If not, how will you change it to try again tomorrow?

_____

_____

❀ What were some challenges that came up today?

_____

_____

❀ How can you use a different lens (objectively) to see this situation differently?

_____

❀ What were some tips/tricks that you tried today? What worked and didn't work?

_____

_____

❀ Can you think of why they may have not worked? What would you change?

_____

_____

❀ Who was there for you today when you needed them?

_____

❀ How did you practice being assertive today? How did it feel?

_____

_____

❀ What was a proud moment for you today?

_____

_____

❀ What are you grateful for today?

_____

✿ Date:
_____

✿ What new goal or intention did you set out to try today?

_____

✿ Did you achieve it? If not, how will you change it to try again tomorrow?

_____

_____

✿ What were some challenges that came up today?

_____

_____

✿ How can you use a different lens (objectively) to see this situation differently?

_____

✿ What were some tips/tricks that you tried today? What worked and didn't work?

_____

_____

✿ Can you think of why they may have not worked? What would you change?

_____

_____

✿ Who was there for you today when you needed them?

_____

✿ How did you practice being assertive today? How did it feel?

_____

_____

✿ What was a proud moment for you today?

_____

_____

✿ What are you grateful for today?

_____

❀ Date:

_____

❀ *Day 25*

❀ What new goal or intention did you set out to try today?

_____

❀ Did you achieve it? If not, how will you change it to try again tomorrow?

_____

_____

❀ What were some challenges that came up today?

_____

_____

❀ How can you use a different lens (objectively) to see this situation differently?

_____

❀ What were some tips/tricks that you tried today? What worked and didn't work?

_____

_____

❀ Can you think of why they may have not worked? What would you change?

_____

_____

❀ Who was there for you today when you needed them?

_____

❀ How did you practice being assertive today? How did it feel?

_____

_____

❀ What was a proud moment for you today?

_____

_____

❀ What are you grateful for today?

_____

❀ Date:
_____

❀ What new goal or intention did you set out to try today?

_____

❀ Did you achieve it? If not, how will you change it to try again tomorrow?

_____

_____

❀ What were some challenges that came up today?

_____

_____

❀ How can you use a different lens (objectively) to see this situation differently?

_____

❀ What were some tips/tricks that you tried today? What worked and didn't work?

_____

_____

❀ Can you think of why they may have not worked? What would you change?

_____

_____

❀ Who was there for you today when you needed them?

_____

❀ How did you practice being assertive today? How did it feel?

_____

_____

❀ What was a proud moment for you today?

_____

_____

❀ What are you grateful for today?

_____

❀ Day 26

❀ Date:
_____

❀ Day 27

❀ What new goal or intention did you set out to try today?
_____

❀ Did you achieve it? If not, how will you change it to try again tomorrow?
_____
_____

❀ What were some challenges that came up today?
_____
_____

❀ How can you use a different lens (objectively) to see this situation differently?
_____

❀ What were some tips/tricks that you tried today? What worked and didn't work?
_____
_____

❀ Can you think of why they may have not worked? What would you change?
_____
_____
_____

❀ Who was there for you today when you needed them?
_____
_____

❀ How did you practice being assertive today? How did it feel?
_____
_____
_____

❀ What was a proud moment for you today?
_____
_____
_____

❀ What are you grateful for today?
_____

❀ Date:

_____

❀ What new goal or intention did you set out to try today?

_____

❀ Did you achieve it? If not, how will you change it to try again tomorrow?

_____

_____

❀ What were some challenges that came up today?

_____

_____

❀ How can you use a different lens (objectively) to see this situation differently?

_____

❀ What were some tips/tricks that you tried today? What worked and didn't work?

_____

_____

❀ Can you think of why they may have not worked? What would you change?

_____

_____

❀ Who was there for you today when you needed them?

_____

❀ How did you practice being assertive today? How did it feel?

_____

_____

❀ What was a proud moment for you today?

_____

_____

❀ What are you grateful for today?

_____

Day 28

❀ Date:

_____

❀ What new goal or intention did you set out to try today?

_____

❀ Did you achieve it? If not, how will you change it to try again tomorrow?

_____

_____

❀ What were some challenges that came up today?

_____

_____

❀ How can you use a different lens (objectively) to see this situation differently?

_____

❀ What were some tips/tricks that you tried today? What worked and didn't work?

_____

_____

❀ Can you think of why they may have not worked? What would you change?

_____

_____

_____

❀ Who was there for you today when you needed them?

_____

❀ How did you practice being assertive today? How did it feel?

_____

_____

❀ What was a proud moment for you today?

_____

_____

❀ What are you grateful for today?

_____

Date:

What new goal or intention did you set out to try today?

_____

Did you achieve it? If not, how will you change it to try again tomorrow?

_____

_____

What were some challenges that came up today?

_____

_____

How can you use a different lens (objectively) to see this situation differently?

_____

What were some tips/tricks that you tried today? What worked and didn't work?

_____

_____

Can you think of why they may have not worked? What would you change?

_____

_____

Who was there for you today when you needed them?

_____

How did you practice being assertive today? How did it feel?

_____

_____

What was a proud moment for you today?

_____

_____

What are you grateful for today?

_____

References

BOOKS

Wiseman, Rosalind (2016). Queen Bees and Wannabes, 3rded. New York, NY. Harmony Books.

Guiran, Michael (2002). The Wonder of Girls. New York, NY: Atria Books

Dweck, Carol (2006). Mindset, A New Psychology of Success. New York, NY: Ballantine Books.

Siegel, Daniel (2017). Brainstorm. New York, NY: Penguin Random House Books.

Simmons, Rachel (2002). Odd Girl Out, The Hidden Culture of Aggression in Girls. New York, NY: First Mariner Books.

ARTICLES

Psychological Review (2000). Biobehavioral responses to stress in females: tend-and-befriend, not fight or flight. Volume 107, no. 3, 411-429.

Taylor, Shelley E. (2011). Tend and Befriend Theory in the Handbook of Theories of Social Psychology. Sage Publications. A.M. Van Lange, A.W. Kruglanski, and E.T. Higgins (Eds.)
     Link: https://taylorlab.psych.ucla.edu/wp-content/uploads/sites/5/2014/11/2011_Tend-and-Befriend-Theory.pdf

Marigold Girls website for fun and information!
WWW.MARIGOLDGIRLS.COM

Made in the USA
Middletown, DE
05 October 2021

49461320R00073